THE BUSINESS OF INNOVATING ONLINE

THE BUSINESS OF INNOVATING ONLINE

Practical Tips and Advice From Industry Leaders

Edited by

Kathryn E. Linder

Foreword by Nina B. Huntemann

STERLING, VIRGINIA

COPYRIGHT © 2019 BY STYLUS PUBLISHING, LLC.

Published by Stylus Publishing, LLC.
22883 Quicksilver Drive
Sterling, Virginia 20166-2019

Library of Congress Cataloging-in-Publication Data
Names: Linder, Kathryn E., editor.
Title: The business of innovating online : practical tips and advice from industry leaders / Edited by Kathryn E. Linder ; Foreword by Nina Huntemann.
Description: First edition. | Sterling, Virginia : Stylus Publishing, [2019] | Includes bibliographical references and index.
Identifiers: LCCN 2019017598 (print) | LCCN 2019020073 (ebook) | ISBN 9781620368442 (library networkable e-edition) | ISBN 9781620368459 (consumer e-edition) | ISBN 9781620368428 (cloth : alk. paper) | ISBN 9781620368435 (pbk. : alk. paper)
Subjects: LCSH: Distance education--Administration. | Distance education--Effect of technological innovations on. | Educational innovations. | Education, Higher--Computer-assisted instruction--Administration.
Classification: LCC LC5800 (ebook) | LCC LC5800 .B87 2019 (print) | DDC 374/4--dc23
LC record available at https://lccn.loc.gov/2019017598

13-digit ISBN: 978-1-62036-842-8 (cloth)
13-digit ISBN: 978-1-62036-843-5 (paperback)
13-digit ISBN: 978-1-62036-844-2 (library networkable e-edition)
13-digit ISBN: 978-1-62036-845-9 (consumer e-edition)

Printed in the United States of America

All first editions printed on acid-free paper that meets the American National Standards Institute Z39-48 Standard.

Bulk Purchases

Quantity discounts are available for use in workshops and for staff development.
Call 1-800-232-0223

First Edition, 2019

For all the online teaching and learning innovators who are changing higher education for the better

CONTENTS

BOXES AND FIGURES

Boxes

Figures

Online education has experienced tremendous growth in the last decade: The number of students participating in fully online and blended learning has increased, the range of courses and programs available has broadened, the types of degrees and credentials awarded have multiplied, and the investment in educational technologies to support online teaching and learning has exploded. In 2012, massive open online courses (MOOCs) captured international attention, furthering conversations on college campuses about the future of education. Tens of millions of people now learn online through digital platforms, like edX, that support MOOCs and online learning at scale.

Often missing from discussions about the expansion of online education is the hard work and commitment, deft organizational management, and difficult cultural change required to design, launch, and sustain a successful online education business. As head of academics and research at edX, I get to collaborate with innovative people and organizations from all over the world, including a good number of the contributors and institutions represented in this book. The work of designing and delivering quality online education to millions of learners worldwide attracts risk-embracing, imaginative, experimentation-minded trailblazers who do not shy away from hard challenges. However, as I have seen, such attributes exist in concert with a deep understanding and respect for academic cultures, pragmatism and analytical decision-making, and the courage to pivot or shut down unsuccessful initiatives.

Much has been written about the need to transform higher education for the digital age, but far less exists that demonstrates how to do it. This book and the chapters herein fill that gap by providing case studies, conversations, and frameworks for innovation. For global society to solve the pressing issues of the twenty-first century, we require a rapid and exponential increase in access to quality education. The educators included in this book have been at the forefront of some of the boldest initiatives developed to meet this urgent need. I am encouraged by their accomplishments as well as the lessons they have learned and share here.

I look forward to the innovations and inventions that their stories and perspectives inspire in you.

Nina B. Huntemann
Senior Director of Academics and Research
edX
January 2019

ACKNOWLEDGMENTS

This book would not have been possible without the help of many people. I wish to first thank the contributors to this volume, who have tirelessly worked on their contributions over many months and drafts. This book was created from the knowledge and experiences of these dedicated online learning leaders.

Our editors at Stylus Publishing, Sarah Burrows and David Brightman, have directed the creation of this volume with flexibility, grace, and helpful critical questions. Amy Donley, whose attention to detail made this volume great, spent many hours copy editing and formatting the chapters (however, any remaining mistakes are certainly my responsibility).

A special thank-you to Rolin Moe, Thomas Cavanagh, Luke Dowden, and Rovy Branon, who answered my request to provide contributions much later in the process in hopes of blending additional important perspectives into this volume. They are exemplary colleagues who were able to produce amazing work in a short period of time.

I owe a great deal of appreciation to the members of the Oregon State University Ecampus leadership team, many of whom contributed to chapters in this volume, for their support throughout this project. A special thank-you to Lisa L. Templeton, who allowed me to carve out the time and space needed for this edited collection among many other projects and priorities.

INTRODUCTION

Kathryn E. Linder

Kanter (2013) argues that innovation is "never a fad, but [is] always in or out of fashion" (p. 101). I think it is safe to say that in contemporary higher education, innovation is currently in fashion, especially in online education, where the sands of educational technology are constantly shifting under our feet. For almost 10 years, the concept of *disruptive innovation* has been a buzzword in higher education (Christensen, Horn, & Johnson, 2008). Advancing cultures of innovation has been a key trend in the last 3 years of the New Media Consortium horizon reports (Adams Becker, Cummins, Davis, Freeman, Hall Giesinger, & Ananthanarayanan, 2017; Johnson, Adams Becker, Cummins, Estrada, Freeman, & Hall, 2016; Johnson, Adams Becker, Estrada, & Freeman, 2015). In 2015 EDUCAUSE released a report titled "Building a Culture of Innovation in Higher Education" (Setser & Morris, 2015). However, even if we can all agree that we should be engaging in innovations at our institutions, the logistics of creating a culture of innovation, systematically implementing innovations, and assessing the success or failure of particular innovations is easier said than done.

The Three Horizons Framework

A helpful model when thinking about innovation in the context of higher education is that of Baghai, Coley, and White (2000), who describe three main stages, or horizons, of a business life cycle and argue that each of these stages "calls for radically different business initiatives . . . [and] poses a different management challenge" (p. 4). The three horizon framework is useful for thinking about businesses within businesses, such as the online education organizations that develop in institutions of higher education. Perhaps most useful is that the framework can be scaled in such a way that it can be applied to higher education institutions and to the online education units that have developed within those institutions (see Figure I.1). In this section I elaborate on each of the horizons and discuss why this framework can offer a foundation for thinking about the business of innovating online.

Horizon 1 includes the core components of a business. For a higher education institution, this might include the programs, courses, and

1

Figure I.1. Applying the three horizons framework to a higher education institution.

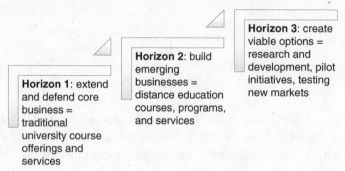

services that have been associated with the institution from its inception or just the elements that the institution has become known for over time. These core elements have a strong relationship with the institution's overall brand and identity and are a central component of the overall profit of the institution. Components of a Horizon 1 business might still be growing but will eventually plateau. For example, many higher education institutions have seen their enrollments level off or have facility constraints that do not allow enrollments to continue to grow over time. However, the revenue from the core elements of the Horizon 1 business will fund Horizons 2 and 3 (more on these later).

Interestingly, the concept of a Horizon 1 business can be scaled down to apply to areas in a higher education institution as well. For example, the framework can be applied to a more mature online education organization. It is possible that online education organizations have programs and courses that are their bread and butter in terms of revenue. Similarly, online education organizations may have certain core elements such as customer service, continuous innovation, or revenue-sharing models that have become part of their institutional identity. These core elements of the online education organization will help to fund the Horizon 2 and 3 initiatives.

Baghai and colleagues (2000) describe Horizon 2 businesses as "on the rise: fast-moving, entrepreneurial ventures in which a concept is taking root or growth is accelerating" (p. 5). These businesses are necessarily nimbler and more reactive to market forces but also need considerable investments to be successful. In many institutions of higher education, the online education organization fits this description, which is why it can sometimes be compared with a start-up. Although Horizon 2 businesses may not be immediately profitable, they should eventually rival the core business elements of Horizon 1 in terms of revenue. Whether Horizon 2 is an extension of Horizon 1, or moves an institution in an entirely new direction, the main focus is on creating new forms of revenue. Just as with Horizon 1, online education organizations can also apply this framework in their work. In addition to the core elements of the online education organization, a constant reinvestment of resources in new areas of growth such as new programs, courses, and services will keep the organization competitive in a shifting market.

Horizon 3 is centered on looking to the future. Baghai and colleagues (2000) describe Horizon 3 as including "research projects, test-market pilots, alliances, minority stakes, and memoranda of understanding that mark the first steps toward actual businesses, even though they may not produce profits for a decade, if ever" (p. 6). Horizon 3 is where businesses will assume the most risk because there is no assurance of a payoff for the different investments that might be made in these exploratory projects. For some institutions, the creation of an online education organization represents a Horizon 3 project in itself. In online education organizations, Horizon 3 investments, given current technologies, might include research and development in virtual and augmented reality, adaptive and personalized learning platforms, and wearable technologies, among other innovative directions.

Baghai and colleagues (2000) argue that for a business to be successful, it "must maintain a continuous pipeline of business-building initiatives. Only if it keeps the pipeline full will it have new growth engines ready when existing ones begin to falter" (p. 1). This means that the maintenance of each of the business horizons described here is not carried out sequentially but simultaneously. The core elements of the business must be nurtured and supported even as the more innovative and riskier ventures are funded and explored. Online education organizations looking to expand, innovate, and scale their business must be prepared to do the complicated work of juggling each of these areas. If Horizon 1 is not strong enough, then the investments needed for Horizons 2 and 3 will not be sufficient. If Horizons 2 or 3 are empty, it may be that innovation, and the revenue that innovation might provide, is not being supported appropriately.

The Business of Innovating Online

This kind of application of a business framework such as the three horizons to the innovative work of an online education organization is not new. Indeed, it is not uncommon for online education organizations to be compared with start-ups in that they are expected to be nimble with idea generation and execution, be customer centered, and operate in a highly competitive market. Throughout this volume, the online education leaders who have contributed chapters provide a range of perspectives for how they have shaped their online education organizations in business-minded frameworks to enhance innovation.

As we begin to explore the business of innovating online, it can be helpful to look at definitions of the term *innovation* from the following sources:

- Drucker (2013) describes innovation as "the effort to create purposeful, focused change in an enterprise's economic or social potential" (p. 143).
- Keeley, Pikkel, Quinn, and Walters (2013) describe innovation as "the creation of a viable new offering" (p. 5).
- Terwiesch and Ulrich (2009) describe innovation as "a new match between a need and a solution" (p. 3).
- For Tucker (2002), innovation is "coming up with ideas and bringing them to life" (p. 18).

What each of these definitions have in common is the pattern of connecting innovation to change, newness, and creation. Each of the contributors throughout the volume discuss innovation through this lens.

The challenge many online education organizations face is that they must innovate and move quickly to stay competitive while being simultaneously situated in the traditional space of academia. In chapter 1, "Strategies to Advance Innovation in Online Education: Eight Lessons Learned at Penn State World Campus," Craig D. Weidemann responds to this tension. Drawing heavily from the work of business strategist Jim Collins, Weidemann offers lessons learned while expanding Penn State World Campus. In particular, he shares tactics for aligning the work of an online organization with a traditional campus and discusses how to balance and align the innovative vision of an online organization with the more traditional aims of the larger institution. Govindarajam and Trimble (2013) refer to this tension as the *innovation wars* in which those tasked with innovations are isolated from, and sometimes pitted against, those working on the day-to-day operations of an organization. Instead, they recommend "a partnership between a dedicated team and the performance engine" (p. 12) to aid in the execution of innovation across a range of organization types. In this chapter, Weidemann offers a real-life example of how this kind of partnership can develop and thrive.

The rapid and ongoing development of online education models requires institutions of higher education to continually innovate to meet the needs of diverse students and industry stakeholders. At the same time, online education organizations require a stable vision to guide their work. In chapter 2, "Establishing a Vision for Innovation," Shannon Riggs, Lisa L. Templeton,

Alfonso Bradoch, Jessica DuPont, Dianna Fisher, and Kathryn E. Linder, all from Oregon State University's Ecampus, share strategies for drafting a vision that makes room for innovation and for implementing and shifting that vision as the online organization grows. Using the example of the innovation vision that has guided the Oregon State University Ecampus, the contributors provide a series of reflective prompts to help readers identify and clarify their own organizational visions for innovation.

Drucker (2013) offers a model of seven key areas where innovative opportunities can be found: unexpected occurrences, incongruities, process needs, industry and market changes, demographic changes, changes in perception, and new knowledge. Without purposefully seeking opportunities to innovate, Drucker (2013) argues that entrepreneurial ventures will struggle to stay ahead in the marketplace. As online education organizations grow and develop, "distance education leaders increasingly are asked to innovate in areas that have potentially dramatic impact on other parts of the university community" (Miller et al., 2013, p. 42). This is particularly true with some of the financial models for online organizations, which can look quite different from other revenue generators across an institution. In chapter 3, "Innovative Financial Models," Rovy Branon, Lisa L. Templeton, Nelson C. Baker, and Kathryn E. Linder discuss some of the financial models most common to online education organizations and explore the pros and cons of these models for different higher education institution types and contexts. The contributors also share different methods of encouraging campus administrator to support innovative financial models.

In many online education organizations, innovation goes hand in hand with collaboration. This relationship is further explored in chapter 4, "Innovation via Consortium," by four members of the Unizin Consortium, who represent three institutions. The Unizin Consortium is one example of higher education institutions pooling resources to accomplish a shared goal. In this chapter, Brad Wheeler (Indiana University), James Hilton (University of Michigan), Lois Brooks (Oregon State University), and Dave King (Oregon State University) discuss the challenges and opportunities provided by consortial relationships and particularly for innovations involving technology, teaching, and learning. Although they argue that consortium-like relationships will continue to develop in the future, they also point to the limitations of these relationships for advancing goals quickly.

As Miller and colleagues (2013) note, the growth of online education "has brought into leadership roles academics and other professionals for whom distance education is a new venture and who have little connection with the preexisting distance education community" (p. 3). Thus, the online education administrator community is diverse, with a range of experience levels related to e-learning and the business of innovating online. In chapter 5, "Effectively Leading Innovation," Thomas Cavanagh and Luke Dowden provide an overview of best practices for leaders of online education organizations with a particular focus on nurturing a culture of innovation. Covering such topics as staffing structures, skill development, and metrics for success, they offer a helpful road map for online learning leaders of any experience level.

In chapter 6, "Making Innovation Stick," Phil Regier and Kathryn Scheckel provide a behind-the-scenes view of the collaboration between Arizona State University and Starbucks, arguably one of the most innovative partnerships in online education. This innovation is what Day (2013) would call a "Big I" innovation, that is, an innovation that goes beyond small performance improvement and that is "new to the company or new to the world" (p. 59). In this chapter, the contributors focus on the practical strategies that allow online education organizations to create sustainable innovations that become embedded in an institutional framework and can lead to future creative endeavors.

In addition to the many other factors mentioned previously, innovations in online education must also meet high-quality standards and produce visible outcomes tied to student success. In chapter 7, "Ensuring Quality While Creating and Innovating," Deborah Adair and Kay Shattuck discuss the importance of quality assurance for online education. The contributors offer a comprehensive taxonomy of quality standards that can be applied across a range of online organizations, from those that are young to those that are more mature. This chapter provides clear evidence of the need for a coordinated approach to assessing quality and for continuous efforts of quality assurance across time, initiatives, and organizational units.

The high-pressure conditions of innovation can create cultures of stress in which online education units are challenged to simultaneously focus on the bottom line and on creating the culture of innovation needed to help their programs thrive. This challenging tension necessitates a community of support and resources such as that described in chapter 8, "Supporting Creativity and Innovation Through Professional Development and Community Building." Jill Buban, Cali M.K. Morrison, Karen L. Pedersen, Amy Claire Heitzman, and Julie Uranis, who represent several national organizations that serve the online learning community, discuss the different services, events, and practices their organizations have fostered in support of the online teaching and learning community. Naturally, these organizations have also had to innovate to meet the needs of their members.

Duhigg (2016) argues that creativity "can't be reduced to a formula . . . there is no checklist that, if followed, delivers innovation on demand" (p. 235). Although this may be true, certain practices, cultures, and climates can help foster creativity and innovation. For example, Duhigg said that one way of "jump-starting the creating process [is by] taking proven, conventional ideas from other settings and combining them in new ways" (p. 212). In the conclusion, Rolin Moe and Kathryn E. Linder synthesize all the insights from the previous chapters into a series of shared principles that have worked across institutions to create and support cultures of innovation to further student learning and success in the online environment. This conclusion also points to some of the future directions for the business of innovating online that online learning organization leaders will need to attend to in the decades to come.

Conclusion

The Business of Innovating Online responds to a critical need for concrete narratives of innovation success that can serve as a foundation for online education administrators who are in need of practical guidance as online learning organizations use innovation to scale and grow. As change is occurring across the higher education landscape, this volume offers an increased understanding of the practices, cultures, and climates that support creativity and innovation in the administration of online education programs across institution types. Drucker's (2013) argument that "what innovation requires is hard, focused, purposeful work" (p. 156) is echoed in the stories in this volume. As evident in the following chapters, the business of innovating online is certainly not something that happens by accident.

References

Adams Becker, S., Cummins, M., Davis, A., Freeman, A., Hall Giesinger, C., & Ananthanarayanan, V. (2017). *NMC horizon report: 2017 higher education edition*. Austin, TX: New Media Consortium.

Baghai, M., Coley, S., & White, D. (2000). *The alchemy of growth: Practical insights for building the enduring enterprise*. Cambridge, MA: Perseus.

Christensen, C. M., Horn, M. B., & Johnson, C. W. (2008). How "disruptive innovation" will change the way we learn. *Education Week, 27*(39), 2536.

Day, G. S. (2013). Is it real? Can we win? Is it worth doing? *Harvard Business Review,* 59–81.

Drucker, P. (2013). The discipline of innovation. *Harvard Business Review,* 143–156.

Duhigg, C. (2016). *Smarter, faster, better: The secrets of being productive in life and business*. New York, NY: Random House.

Govindarajam, V., & Trimble, C. (2013). Stop the innovation wars. *Harvard Business Review,* 11–25.

Johnson, L., Adams Becker, S., Cummins, M., Estrada, V., Freeman, A., & Hall, C. (2016). *NMC horizon report: 2016 higher education edition*. Austin, TX: New Media Consortium.

Johnson, L., Adams Becker, S., Estrada, V., & Freeman, A. (2015). *NMC horizon report: 2015 higher education edition*. Austin, TX: New Media Consortium.

Kanter, R. M. (2013). Innovation: The classic traps. *Harvard Business Review*, 101–124.

Keeley, L., Pikkel, R., Quinn, B., & Walters, H. (2013). *Ten types of innovation: The discipline of building breakthroughs*. Hoboken, NJ: Wiley.

Miller, G., Benke, M., Chaloux, B., Ragan, L. C., Schroeder, R., Smutz, W., & Swan, K. (2013). *Leading the e-learning transformation of higher education: Meeting the challenges of technology and distance education*. Sterling, VA: Stylus.

Setser, B., & Morris, H. (2015). Building a culture of innovation in higher education: Design & practice for leaders. Retrieved from https://library.educause.edu/~/media/files/library/2015/4/ngt1502-pdf.pdf

Terwiesch, C., & Ulrich, K. T. (2009). *Innovation tournaments: Creating and selecting exceptional opportunities*. Boston, MA: Harvard Business Press.

Tucker, R. B. (2002). *Driving growth through innovation: How leading firms are transforming their futures*. San Francisco, CA: Berrett-Koehler.

STRATEGIES TO ADVANCE INNOVATION IN ONLINE EDUCATION

Eight Lessons Learned at Penn State World Campus

Craig D. Weidemann

Building an innovative online enterprise that is embedded in the core of an academic institution requires a long-term commitment to persistent cultural change that provides the fertile ground for innovation. Creating a long-term innovative organization is a marathon, not a sprint. This strategy necessitates a fundamental commitment to creating a sustainable innovative online organizational model that fits into the traditional, slow-to-change academic culture while successfully driving innovation to achieve its goals and to ultimately affect and change the institutional core. Dancing among these seemingly conflicting forces is at the center of driving innovation in the academy. Yet that is our challenge. How do you build an innovative online enterprise inside a traditional academic institution?

This chapter uses Penn State World Campus as a case study, showing how the application of the fundamental findings in leadership and management principles in Collins's (2001) seminal research and his related management books (e.g., Collins, 2005; Collins, 2009, Collins & Hansen, 2011; Collins & Porras, 1994) can advance an innovative and sustainable online initiative in a traditional higher education institution. Although we are bombarded with the emerging plethora of the latest books and trends on building an innovative organization or strategy in the public and private sectors, we found concrete foundational and long-term benefits to focusing on the fundamental principles in Collins's (2001) timeless work, now more than 15 years old. Despite its age, the fundamental leadership principles in Collins's extensive research of successful organizations provided the foundation for the innovation and success of the World Campus.

I believe that the unique application of these business principles in a traditional academic institution are an effective strategy to advance the pursuit of innovation. They are also more effective than traditional higher education organizational strategies or following the innovative practice du jour. Throughout this chapter, I provide specific examples as guideposts and lessons learned from Collins's work to enable readers to apply his findings to create a successful online higher education enterprise sustained through the establishment of an innovative culture.

Creating a Culture of Innovation in the Academy

Despite higher education's reputation as a slow, stodgy bureaucracy, innovation is deeply embedded in the academic core of higher education institutions, and it is, in fact, a fundamental value. The focus on discovery is simply central to the foundation of the academic research enterprise and reflects a deep engagement with innovative thinking. As Boyer (2016) states, "The advancement of knowledge can generate an almost palpable excitement in the life of an educational institution" (p. 69). However, the ubiquitous nature of the innovation and discovery process rooted in the academic research community is in contrast to the inherent, cumbersome bureaucratic administrative—and some academic—practices deeply entrenched throughout higher education. Higher education's traditional administrative and academic practices frequently eschew change.

For example, many institutions have been slow to adopt new entrance requirements for adult students, accept competency-based instruction and microcredentials, expedite the transfer credit approval process, embrace prior learning assessment, engage with private sector educational technology firms to augment student facing and external services, and implement student assistance 24 hours a day, 7 days a week. Unfortunately, often our services are designed for our own internal legacy operations, not the high and immediate service expectations of our students. A simple problem with a tuition bill can send a student on a sojourn from the admissions office to the registrar to the advising office to the financial aid office to the bursar.

Despite a bevy of external factors—changing demographics of our student body, concerns with escalating costs and student debt, emerging disruption of technology in every sector, and the growing incongruence between our graduates' skills and employers' needs—the overall higher education enterprise reflects an ongoing reluctance to embrace the need for change and innovation. Perhaps the longevity of the higher education sector, with some institutional lineages dating from the 1600s, encourages a culture of tradition rather than adaptation. In fact, 25 institutions celebrate academic pedigrees of more than 300 years of existence. This incredible legacy of endurance solidifies higher education's self-perceived lack of the need for nimbleness or an urgency to change. As a result, it is extremely difficult to engage in any major institutional change in a higher education enterprise. Efforts to advance change in the academy are frequently thwarted by legacy practices and policies, many of which neither serve their original purpose nor have adapted to our changing world.

Lessons Learned From Implementing the World Campus

So how do leaders advance innovations in a bureaucratic organization like higher education? I believe the core strategy demands that leaders focus on fundamentally creating a culture of innovation. And I believe that closely adhering to the disciplined application of the simple, but profound, findings of Collins's (2001, 2005, 2009) work in his well-researched organizational leadership books can provide the critical long-term foundation to advance this innovative organization in the larger academy. The sustained success of the World Campus, rated the number one online bachelor's program and the number one military-friendly institution (*Penn State News*, 2015a, 2015b), with all World Campus online programs ranked in the top 10, reinforces this assumption. The World Campus—now with every academic college offering at least 1 of more than 130 undergraduate and graduate academic programs, a well-established community of more than 200 learning designers, double-digit growth for 10 consecutive years, and 18,000 plus students—benefitted from Collin's (2001) well-researched assessment of the foundational principles for building sustainable organizations.

The World Campus, established in 1993 under the leadership of President Graham Spanier and aided by a significant gift from the Alfred P. Sloan Foundation, began with 4 academic programs and 40 students. At the time, the number of online providers across higher education was limited, and many institutions jumped into the online delivery of education by creating for-profit entities, separate from the core academy. Penn State pursued a very different path, which most importantly aligned our strategy with the Penn State culture. The World Campus was built on two traditions, the first of which is Penn State's long-term legacy commitment to providing access to world-class education to students across the Commonwealth of Pennsylvania and around the globe, a core principle of its land-grant mission. Penn State had a historic commitment to distance education, which began in 1885 with rural, free delivery courses that evolved to correspondence courses and later offerings through satellite television.

The second tradition is that from its inception, the World Campus also made a commitment to offer a Penn State degree online, with the same admission requirements, same faculty, and same academic programs as a traditional on-campus Penn State degree. This centralized online learning model ensured that the World Campus offered programs that were deeply embedded in the core academy and engaged students who wanted to obtain a rigorous, quality Penn State education from a distance. This principle proved to be a very sound strategy for Penn State, but it did result in a much slower growth trajectory as the entire academy needed to be involved with the new innovative delivery enterprise.

I arrived in 2003 as vice president of outreach to oversee the largest unified outreach organization in higher education, including the World Campus, established four years earlier. Our leadership team immediately began to implement Collins's (2001) core principles in the World Campus and in outreach. I had previous experience with the assimilation of Collins's findings at my former institution, the University of Maryland, Baltimore County, where we implemented his principles under the tutelage of a university advisory board member, Ed Ludwig, then CEO of Becton Dickinson, a global multibillion-dollar medical technology company. He was a fervent believer in the effectiveness of Collins's organizational leadership findings from his experience with applying them at Becton Dickinson.

After my arrival at Penn State, Ludwig and I began our interaction with Collins and his work. Collins shared our interest in applying his findings to the education sector, K–12 and higher education, and he assessed our organization and consulted with our core management team to help us consider this strategic process. In his research, Collins and his colleagues (Collins & Porras, 1994; Collins & Hansen, 2011) slowly and thoughtfully built all their findings on a deep assessment of significant longitudinal organizational data and not on anecdotal outcomes. He and his research team operated with no hypothesis regarding expected success variables. Instead, they followed where the data took them, not where they wanted the data to go. Their methodological approach to advance well-researched, not flashy, and thoughtful strategies aligns and is congruent with the academic culture of higher education.

That being said, higher education leaders are not inclined to follow a specific management orientation, especially one grounded in research from the private sector. It is my experience that the higher education enterprise frequently disregards consideration of private sector business practices, claiming that higher education is not a business. However, Collins (2005) addressed this perception and presented examples of his findings being applied and adopted by many nonprofit organizations. Unlike some organizational innovation strategies that focus on disruptive innovations or blowing up old models, Collins advanced the axiom that sustainable innovative organizations did not chase the newest shining technology or management trend but rather pursued a long-term commitment to creating an organization steeped in social innovation. That is, the elements of innovation were socialized deeply into the organizational core. Fundamentally, he found that being innovative required a deep commitment to creating an environment that would become a seedbed for many insanely great innovations in the short and long term, in contrast to creating frequent, isolated innovations built on tactical short-term initiatives often with little expectations of survival.

Lesson 1: Protect the Legacy Core While Pursuing Innovation

Collins (1994) wrote that successful companies tenaciously adhere to a foundational principle of pursuing a strategy that balances preserving core legacy principles as an organizational anchor point while simultaneously stimulating change, innovation, and renewal in everything else. This tension of protecting the core while pursuing innovation is central to the success of the World Campus. In fact, back in the 1990s, when a number of universities created separate for-profit enterprises to house their online learning initiatives, Penn State pursued the much slower strategy of building an online enterprise deeply embedded in the academy with the same faculty, same academic programs, and same admission requirements as the traditional campus—again, protecting the core while achieving innovation. Another example at Penn State of the nuance of balancing tradition with innovation happened at the beginning of the online program. While the university pursued the nascent and untested delivery of online education through the World Campus, the administration created the university-wide World Campus Steering Committee governing body, composed of the university's key academic leaders, to ensure the preservation of the World Campus's academic integrity and quality. The Steering Committee established the innovative World Campus revenue-sharing model that allowed our academic deans to generate significant discretionary dollars to fund core academic priorities (e.g., travel, equipment, graduate assistants, etc.), and in times of budget cuts to provide funding to ensure the university maintains its focus on world-class quality. This revenue-sharing model continues to operate today.

Lesson 2: Pursuit of Innovation Must Align With the Core Institutional Culture

One of the most salient points in this chapter is the critical importance of ensuring that the pursuit of innovation in the academy aligns with what the individual institution can bear. Leaders violating this principle may be perceived as pursuing innovation for innovation's sake, or worse they may be perceived as the enemy and out of touch with what is acceptable organizational change.

Operationally, the World Campus approached advancing innovation under the threshold of innovation at Penn State. That is, we did not operate outside the box but rather pushed out the walls of the box. I contend that in 1993 when the World Campus originated, it probably was significantly ahead of the core thinking of the university on stimulating progress. However, in 2016 I believe the World Campus moved into the core of the institution, with every college and most Penn State campuses offering their academic programs through the World Campus. Also, many innovative academic practices and administrative processes, some derived from the private sector, that originated in the World Campus were moved to the traditional institution. Again, the most notable point is that the World Campus was always operating inside the culture of the university and did not exceed the institution's threshold for innovation.

However, for the World Campus to survive, it is imperative that it continue to aggressively stimulate progress but always within the Penn State culture and always considering what is next to ensure its viability. For example, to consider what is next, we established the Center for Online Innovations in Learning, funded through a percentage of revenues from the World Campus. The center is jointly led by faculty, administrators, and World Campus leaders to fund innovative faculty initiatives and new product development through refereed pilot projects, to invite global innovative leaders for lectures and consultations, and to pursue new major grants that advance innovations in teaching and learning. In addition, in our university-wide Invent Penn State economic development initiative, we are promoting the local educational technology sector by fostering the development of new educational technologies through student and faculty entrepreneurship; creating a for-profit company to advance innovation and aggressively pursue what is next relative to microcredentials, badges, and portfolios; and engaging external private sector educational technology partners to colocate near the university. Finally, we are pursuing an aggressive student engagement initiative to help with the challenge of retention of online adult learners. For example, we are building a collaboration with our alumni association to engage its members through various emerging online mentoring technologies to help the World

Campus students immediately benefit from the largest dues-paying alumni association in higher education and immediately benefit from this very valuable professional network.

Lesson 3: The Power of Pursuing Strategic Pilots

Collins (2001) found that companies did not focus on being innovative as a core strategy but rather elegantly blended creativity with discipline. Rather than jumping in and investing in the pursuit of every new innovation, institution administrators should be judicious and modest in the pursuit of riskier new strategies—in other words, they should be disciplined. He found that sustainable companies invested in pursuing small calculated risks (i.e., shooting small bullets rather than shooting cannons). We employed the strategy of empirical creativity over the years through the ongoing pursuit of rigorous pilot tests to evaluate the implementation of new technologies and services (e.g., coaching, student authentication, tutoring, etc.), especially when working in partnership with private sector organizations. It also drove our modest, but tested, foray into the strategic assessment of providing massive open online courses and the creation of an online student union using Second Life, an online 3D virtual platform. Both endeavors were heavily assessed and provided huge lessons and the foundation for current new endeavors (e.g., Second Life is informing our work using artificial intelligence and virtual reality to improve the student experience). It is critical for these bullets to be low cost; low risk; and most important, low in distraction. We found it is always important to monitor the tolerance for pilots across the organization. Frequently, we have elected not to test, or to delay testing new innovations, because of *pilot fatigue* (i.e., the pilot becomes too much of a distraction for the organization to do its core work).

Lesson 4: Benefits of Findings From Collins (2001)

Penn State's chosen strategy significantly affected the early enrollment and revenue growth of the World Campus as this budding entrepreneurial venture was incubated in a very successful traditional research institution. However, the structure was congruent with our culture. First, it was embedded in our academic core, with the same academic programs, same admission requirements, and same faculty. Second, our organizational model aligned with Christensen's (2011) findings that for unique innovations in large organizations to succeed, they must be either formed separately outside the organization or created as a unique, protected organization (like the World Campus) in the larger institution. That being said, the model did not immunize the World Campus in its early years from significant and aggressive organizational challenges from many traditional academic and administrative practices as we worked to stimulate progress. However, as we integrated many of the principles from Collins's writings, our original strategy was aligned with the core findings in Collins (2001); it not only provided the foundation for our strategy but also created a common management lexicon that allowed the World Campus to communicate quickly and effectively across the organization and among the members of our leadership team.

Collins's (2001) research team identified 11 companies that had 15 years of cumulative stock returns at or below the market, followed by a transition period and a further 15 years with cumulative stock returns 3 times as high as the general stock market (i.e., good to great companies). The team identified an additional 11 companies from the same sectors that did not achieve this level of sustained success. After a thorough assessment of the extensive quantitative and qualitative data, Collins's research team determined a framework of foundational concepts to be critical to the success of good to great companies: a definition of *greatness*, advanced leadership structures, having the right people, and disciplined thought.

Lesson 5: The Power of Defining Greatness

The first foundational concept was truly defining *greatness*, which is the key process of involving everyone in the organization in answering the question, What does it mean to be great? This communication process pushes organizations to move beyond the obvious, traditional, and easy metrics and really focus on how an organization defines greatness. The power of this conversation among colleagues urges everyone to think deeply about what success and excellence truly are. In fact, the process of this rich dialogue is really the product. Over time, the World Campus has pivoted from its original measures of greatness. For example, our early metric was ensuring that online learning was as good as face-to-face instruction. We are in the process of developing new key performance indicators that focus on great learning, student engagement, reducing time to degree, and student success, shifting away from the old quality measure of the traditional classroom.

Lesson 6: Identifying Real Leadership

Collins (2011) found that good to great companies were helmed by leaders entrenched with a deep humility, a willingness to diffuse power, and a fierce tenacity to succeed. These leaders were grounded in the tactic of looking through a window to recognize any organizational triumph and holding up a mirror regarding responsibility for any failing in the organization. Coupled with this humility and responsibility was an unfailing conviction in their organization's success. A commitment that withstands any failings or challenges—failure is simply not an option. This manifested itself in the early years of the World Campus—our team regularly felt as if we were pushing a boulder up a hill, with frequent return visits as it rolled back over us, losing any small wins or advantages. We learned that tenacity is at the core of pushing innovation and the critical importance of working as a team and sharing responsibility.

Lesson 7: Prioritizing Getting and Retaining the Right People

The most important concept from Collins's (2001) research centered on finding the right disciplined people to lead an organization. Every leader knows the most important factor in success is hiring the right people, but Collins offered a new lens on this strategy. He found that successful companies did not hire people for their specific abilities or to align and support specific strategies. He found that the simple key factor in successful hires is focusing on hiring the right people, with the implication that the organizational strategy will change, and the right people will have the attitude and skill sets to not only adopt the new strategy but also provide leadership to achieve the new direction (i.e., determining who, then what). The key is to find people aligned with the core values of the organization and to ensure that they are assigned work congruent with their skills. To drive innovation, it is imperative to apply this strategy religiously.

In nonacademic positions (e.g., marketing, information technology, customer relationship management [CRM], etc.) in the World Campus, the right person is frequently from the private sector. Clearly, that person has to be comfortable with migrating to the very different world of higher education. The value of adding a person with a significant private sector lens to our marketing team or finance group is immeasurable. They not only bring in new perspectives but also advance a culture that is comfortable with the need for speed, nimbleness, and outsourcing or partnerships with educational technology companies that could advance unique new strategies (e.g., CRM, virtual reality project management, etc.). Having colleagues that are willing to move inside the organization to optimize their role to achieve success is the key of any innovative organization. Because of the traditional orientation of human resource practices in higher education of compensation and dismissal, it took many years for the World Campus to secure the right people on the right bus and in the right seats.

Taking the aggressive stance of dismissing staff or helping to move them to the right position inside or outside the organization is not common in higher education, or in many cases anywhere in the public sector, but is absolutely necessary for a high-performing organization. Collins (2001) found the critical strategy is to hire slowly, and when in doubt, do not hire. He also discovered that successful leaders quickly dismiss employees who are not aligned with the organizational direction. From my experience, to retain outstanding talent, especially with the end of the long-term employment covenant between employees and employers, our job as leaders in an innovative organization is to give our colleagues a series of interesting gigs to keep them engaged and challenged. That is, we must constantly provide opportunities for professional growth and the development of new marketable skill sets. Some leaders fear that providing training for strong employees will encourage them to pursue other positions outside the organization; however, the alternative is to ensure they do not learn new skills and remain stagnant and ensure that they never have an opportunity to leave.

Lesson 8: The Importance of Disciplined Focus

Long-term successful organizations do not chase the latest technology. Rather, these companies operate more like a lumbering, slow hedgehog, driven by the singular concept of three questions: What are you deeply passionate about? What drives your economic engine or resource engine (i.e., time, brand, and money)? What can you be best at in the world? Early in the World Campus, we spent a great deal of time wrestling with answering these three core strategic questions. First, we knew that we are deeply passionate about serving the educational needs of adult learners. Second, we created a business model that was self-supported and advanced the goals of the university (i.e., drove our economic engine). Third, we believed we could offer online programs that were the best in the country. We focused on this hedgehog concept, forgoing those initiatives that did not align with this central tenet. For example, we ultimately moved away from any face-to-face programming and instruction and solely focused on offering all instruction through online offerings. In fact, we expected World Campus leaders to include in their annual performance goals the arduous task of identifying and eliminating a legacy process or initiative by creating a *stop-doing* goal.

Another example of adherence to our hedgehog concept is reflected by our disciplined market research practices to determine if we should offer a new program online. We developed a thorough nine-step market research process that captured and evaluated many different elements (e.g., our academic reputation, the academic department's readiness to offer the program, the employment and income potential for graduates, sustainability of the market, and scalability) before we would offer the program (i.e., drive our economic engine). We provide more than 130 fully online undergraduate and graduate programs and have had very few program failures. That being said, we also encouraged failing forward, failing fast, or pivoting after failure. This strategy allowed our colleagues to pursue new initiatives without concern for retaliation or blame. Creating a blameless environment provides the speed of trust that catapults innovation, knowing some innovations are going to fail but can be opportunities for learning. Many years ago, we introduced a process to evaluate new opportunities; it failed miserably. However, after we conducted a blameless autopsy (Collins, 2005) years later, we found the learning provided the foundation for our new Enterprise Project Management Office, which has built our new assessment process to systematically consider the pursuit of all new initiatives.

The success of the World Campus in continually reinventing itself through innovation is not a result of a focus on innovation but rather a by-product of creating an organization, or a culture, with a high level of social innovation. Our experience in the World Campus reinforces the notion that to ensure sustained innovation, we must begin with building a culture of innovation.

References

Boyer, E. (2016). *Scholarship reconsidered: Priorities of the professoriate*. San Francisco, CA: Jossey-Bass.

Christensen, C. (2011). *The innovator's dilemma*. New York, NY: Harper Business.

Collins, J. (2001). *Good to great*. New York, NY: Harper Business.

Collins, J. (2005). *Good to great for the social sectors*. New York, NY: Harper Business.

Collins, J. (2009). *How the mighty fail*. New York, NY: Harper Business.

Collins, J., & Hansen, M. T. (2011). *Great by choice: Uncertainty, chaos, and luck; Why some thrive despite them all*. New York, NY: HarperCollins.

Collins, J., & Porras, J. I. (1994). *Built to last: Successful habits of visionary companies*. New York, NY: Harper Business.

Penn State News. (2015a, January 7). *Penn State online bachelor's programs ranked No. 1 by U.S. News and World Report*. Retrieved from https://news.psu.edu/story/339735/2015/01/07/academics/penn-state-online-bachelors-programs-ranked-no-1-us-news-and-world

Penn State News. (2015b, May 19). *Penn State World Campus undergraduate programs ranked No. 1 for veterans*. Retrieved from https://news.psu.edu/story/358097/2015/05/19/academics/penn-state-world-campus-undergraduate-programs-ranked-no-1

2

ESTABLISHING A VISION
FOR INNOVATION

*Shannon Riggs, Lisa L. Templeton, Alfonso Bradoch, Jessica DuPont,
Dianna Fisher, and Kathryn E. Linder*

Increasingly, institutions of higher learning are claiming innovation as part of their missions and identities. Some have developed centers for innovation, innovation labs, and innovation teams. Others find innovation more elusive and aspirational, especially when faced with constraints on time and resources. In establishing and sustaining a vision for innovation at Oregon State University's Ecampus, we have found it helpful to consider innovation from several perspectives. First, what is a vision and what does it mean to create one for innovation? Second, what is the purpose of a vision for innovation? Third, what are the ways a vision can be made actionable over time? In this chapter, we offer some guidance based on our own experiences and what we have learned over the years, first in establishing an innovative vision for online education and later in sustaining that vision for our Ecampus organization at Oregon State University.

What Is a Vision?

There are many different ways to think about creating and having a vision for your organization. At the core, having a vision for your organization means having a clear understanding of your identity, your purpose, and what you are working toward. Visions, and more specifically vision statements, tend to have several characteristics you may find helpful to keep in mind as you craft your organization's vision for innovation.

Vision Components

Organizational visions are future thinking. When drafting your vision statement, you should think 5, 10, or even 20 years into the future about what your organization might become. Although this can present challenges—indeed, we do not know what the future will hold—it also ensures that your vision is focused on where your organization is going rather than simply where you are right now. That said, organizational visions are not always written down. Although vision statements can certainly be written down and distributed, some of the best vision statements are memorable enough to not be posted around the office. Key components of your vision statement can be embedded in your strategic goals, your organizational mission, and into all parts of your organization that touch innovation. It may also be that you are living your innovation vision without having actually articulated it yet.

Vision statements are aspirational. They can provide leadership for an entire organization and can influence the goals and investments made over time. By aiming high, a vision can stretch and challenge members of an organization to their fullest capacity and can even bring about complete reinvention in some circumstances.

Vision statements are motivational. Providing leadership and direction is important, but equally important is inspiring staff and partners to help make the vision a reality. For a vision statement to be applied, it must energize those who are meant to make it happen. Vision statements can increase the support for a vision and motivate those who are carrying out the vision by creating community and a shared purpose.

Vision statements include everyone in the organization. Although some might think vision statements are just for leaders of an organization to implement and use for guidance, we recommend including all members of your organization in forming and living your vision for innovation. There will be more power in the vision if it is applied across an organization rather than by just a few key people.

Organizational visions move to action quickly and regularly. The most future-thinking, aspirational, motivational vision statement will languish if it is not supported by action. To be sustainable, vision statements must be actionable, which means they are often tied to goals, strategic plans, and action items. You will want to align your vision statements with the actionable steps needed for your organization to be a successful innovator.

Creating a Vision for Innovation

Perhaps because of its inherent characteristics of novelty and inventiveness, *innovation* can be a challenging term to define. Setser and Morris (2015) note that the term is "overused, under-defined and often means something different depending on who you ask" (p. 7). In establishing a vision for innovation at your institution, it will be helpful to define quite specifically what innovation means to you and those with whom you collaborate. Setser and Morris (2015) offer a definition of *innovation* we have found helpful: "the act or process of building on existing research, knowledge, and practice through the introduction or application of new ideas, devices or methods to solve problems or create opportunities where none existed before" (p. 8). We find this definition useful because it encourages thoughtful connection to a specific context, guidance for action, and a purpose.

In the context of our large public university, we see innovation not as a disconnected enterprise or external force but as naturally stemming from the strong foundation of research, knowledge, and instructional practice that are part of our institution's history and identity. As a distance education unit, we see the day-to-day work of innovation as applying new technologies and methods of teaching to bring Oregon State University courses and programs far beyond our campus. Finally, and perhaps most inspirational of all, we see the purpose of innovation as creating opportunities for learners where they did not exist before.

The contextual, practical, and purposeful elements of the Setser and Morris (2015) definition are meaningful and inspiring for us, but others may find additional elements meaningful. As you hone your definition of *innovation*, you might also consider the following: creativity, imagination, results driven, technological, inventiveness, improvement, resourcefulness, sweeping, incremental, unexpected, flexibility, adaptivity, products, processes, novelty, change, value, and growth. Your organization's vision for innovation may vary and, like ours, may evolve over time.

The Purpose of a Vision

When you initially create an innovative vision for online education at your institution, it is helpful to consider the many different ways your vision may have an impact on your unit and your campus as a whole. We have identified six key areas of impact for a vision statement including solving a problem, serving an audience, supporting the university's mission, guiding culture, improving strategic thinking, and strengthening brand identity.

Solving a Problem

In our early days, we saw that many Oregonians were not able to leave their homes, families, and jobs and relocate to Oregon State University's campus to pursue degrees. Access was the principal problem we saw and set out to help solve. Another problem we needed to solve was the need for revenue sufficient to sustain our efforts to bring quality Oregon State University education to learners statewide. As connection speeds and access to the Internet grew, we saw that we could meet the needs of Oregonians better if we developed online courses and degree programs that would allow learners to access education from wherever they resided in the large state of Oregon. Online courses and full degree programs, offered with a creative funding structure (as discussed in chapter 3), became our solution to an access problem and the need for revenue.

Discovering the problem areas in your institution, geographic region, or disciplines is an important step in creating a vision for innovation at your college or university. Consider what is fundamentally broken, flawed, or not working as well as it could be. Problems your constituent student groups might face could include college affordability, a need to balance work and educational pursuits, a desire to minimize childcare needs by pursuing a degree from home, or the need to complete a degree with a job that requires frequent travel or relocation. Problems may also be discipline specific, such as a desire to pursue a degree not offered in a given geographic area. Other problems in need of solution might stem from limitations at your home campus, such as capacity problems, instructor availability challenges that require hiring remote faculty, or other local issues unique to your institution.

Spending some time identifying pain points for students your institution serves may help you develop a vision for innovation. Identifying underserved prospective students or community problems your institution is not yet serving can also be helpful in forming your vision. When your innovations are addressing real needs and problems, your initiatives are likely to garner more support and enthusiasm.

Serving an Audience

Clearly defining your audiences and how your innovative vision affects them will be critical to success in detecting problems and unmet needs. In higher education, there are multiple audiences and needs to consider. Audiences include the following: students, faculty, the institution, and potential employers. Think about the market research you have access to or that you need to obtain to better understand the unmet audience needs and market potential inherent in your innovative vision. You can solve a problem for a small number of people, but to sustain an online education organization, you will need to identify a sizable enough audience, ideally one that will continually replenish itself. In our early history as an organization, there was a large unmet need involving many working adults and parents of young children who wanted to complete their education and were open to online and hybrid educational models. Your institution's potential audience may be similar or may have unique characteristics. Clearly identifying the people your innovative vision will serve is an important early consideration.

For Oregon State University, online education was an innovative way to meet a real need for the people of Oregon who were not able to leave their homes, families, or jobs to earn a degree. By providing greater access to credit-bearing education and the means to earn a degree, we hoped to improve the economic, social, cultural, and environmental opportunities for our constituents. In short, our vision was to use emerging Internet-based technologies and teaching methods to bring Oregon State University degrees, and all the opportunities they offer, to Oregonians statewide.

Supporting the University's Mission

If you can demonstrate that your vision for innovation aligns with and supports your institution's mission and goals, you will be better able to win the cooperation and support of administrators at the highest levels and of partners from across your institution. As a land-grant institution grounded in providing educational access statewide, innovation at Oregon State extends beyond the confines of campus. Innovating in the area of online education was thus a natural fit for Oregon State and felt like a core part of its university mission. Not every institution has a land-grant mission, however. Understanding your institution's larger mission can help you identify what aligns with your vision for innovation in online education. Community colleges often serve working adults, economically disadvantaged populations, students with disabilities, and sometimes incarcerated populations. Institutions located near military bases may have missions that include serving veterans and their families. Some institutions may have missions related to technology that could align with online education initiatives. Others may have religious or spiritual missions that align with a desire to extend the institution's reach. Identifying possible areas of alignment with institutional missions can bring much-needed energy to the creation and maintenance of online programs and can help justify the allocation of resources.

Our early vision for innovation stemmed from our university's mission. As a land-grant institution, Oregon State University (2017) is charged to expand access to education to the people of Oregon to promote economic, social, cultural, and environmental progress. The land-grant mission is the foundation for the university's Extension Service, which brings research-based knowledge to every county statewide through programs such as 4-H, Family and Community Health, and Forestry and Natural Resources. We envisioned online education as a way to build on that land-grant mission.

Guiding Culture

One of the most important outcomes of an innovation vision is the ways this vision can affect a larger institutional culture. For example, an innovation vision can help engage faculty in the online education endeavor. This is equally true for faculty who are the early adopters and beta-testers for online tools and technology innovations and for the faculty who bring problems that need innovative solutions to the door of the online education organization. For both of these faculty groups, providing support to carry out an innovative vision is key.

Having a vision for innovation also includes building a tolerance for risk-taking, missteps, and mistakes. This may be unusual for certain areas of the larger institution and represents one possibility of how online education organizations can provide innovation leadership. Online education organizations can model what it means to be excited about problems, to brainstorm solutions, and to show how problems and challenges can be valued as opportunities—even fun opportunities—for innovation.

Improving Strategic Thinking

To be innovative, you take risks and sometimes fail along the way. Regardless, innovation must be supported by leadership and encouraged throughout the organization. This means leadership understands and expects that problem-solving and creating new opportunities will usually require more than one attempt, and we must try new ways of solving problems as they arise. If innovation is deeply embedded in strategic thinking and planning, occasional missteps and failures will be easier to tolerate, and your organization and employees will be able to recuperate more quickly and effectively.

In our experience, we have certainly experienced missteps and failures. However, because innovation has been woven into our strategic thinking and planning, we have responded to disappointments resiliently rather than feeling discouraged or defeated. For example, one experiment we tried was contracting with an external vendor to expand some of the services we did not yet have the capacity to provide. As we worked with this vendor over time, we discovered that some larger institutional processes outside our organization's purview were not well aligned with the vendor's services, and we made the difficult decision to discontinue the contract. Because we had a clear vision for innovation and a collective tolerance for failed experiments, we were able to focus on lessons learned instead of on the fact that this one venture did not succeed as we had hoped.

Strengthening Brand Identity

In addition to how we know ourselves, and how we can imagine our future, an innovation vision can also strengthen how others know us through our larger brand identity. Understanding how others perceive you internally and externally is foundational to this work. What is your reputation on campus? Do others recognize you and your offerings as innovative? Reviewing recent surveys or developing a new assessment to measure how others perceive you is foundational to understanding your current brand and determining how best to strengthen it through the development of consistent brand identity elements.

Through this kind of work ourselves, we have been able to identify what differentiates our organization and the programs we help deliver in the higher education marketplace. In several ways we have found that what differentiates us from other distance education providers informs our vision for the future. For example, in the state of Oregon, our university is the land-grant institution, which means that it has a unique responsibility among other Oregon public institutions to bring educational opportunities statewide. We have built, and continue to build on, that differentiating aspect of our brand identity to inform our vision of expanding access to education, statewide and beyond.

Another example of the important linkage between one of our market differentiators and our vision began with recognizing that natural resources is a signature strength area for Oregon State University. Based on that differentiator, several successful online natural resource programs have been developed, including our second largest online program in fisheries and wildlife studies. In addition to institution type and signature disciplinary areas, other differentiators that can inform your organization's vision might include programming related to prominent local industries, your institution's reputation for or history with a particular social justice mission, your institution's reputation for attracting students of high academic caliber, your institution's reputation for its commitment to open enrollment, or any reason that compels students to choose your institution over thousands of others. Exploring and understanding which market differentiators your institution possesses is a fruitful place to start to expand your vision.

In addition to investigations of institutional differentiators, your marketing team (either at the institutional level or in your local organization) should routinely audit your existing marketing and communications to find out where you can further strengthen your brand identity. Do your website, press releases, newsletters, and paid media reflect your innovative vision with consistent messaging and design? If your unit is operating in an established university, you are likely tied to the brand guidelines produced by your central marketing office. At a minimum, you should establish or have access to a clear visual identity, such as color palettes, logos, fonts, and consistent styles for photography, illustrations, or image use. If you are building from the ground up, consider consulting with your centralized marketing office on campus to fine-tune how the university's brand can be used to better reflect your unit and vision.

Ultimately, brand guidelines set forth by your unit or the university should delineate a clear brand positioning statement and a creative platform. In addition to creative assets, providing examples of consistent messaging and storytelling are key (e.g., personality traits, tone, and editorial style). Storytelling provides more latitude to emphasize and define the voice and innovative personality of a unit or department. How can you talk about or show your innovative vision through words and creative assets?

At Oregon State Ecampus, we have always recognized the value and our link to the mothership, Oregon State University. However, we have also struggled with the university's brand at times because our audience and programs are not bound to the physical campus founded in 1868. In 2017 the university hired an outside firm to establish and develop a new brand platform after several months of focus groups and surveys among stakeholders. Ecampus ultimately hired the same firm to engage in sub-branding work to build on our unique version of the key personality traits and brand positioning statement that works with our product and audience, namely, top-ranked online degrees and adult learners.

Whether you do this work on your own or outsource it, it is imperative to build in your own assessments along the way to gauge stakeholder perception of your brand; if not, you risk losing sight of the progress you are making and the areas you need to improve on that will ensure a strong brand identity in an increasingly competitive marketplace where multiple providers are claiming to be innovative.

Making Your Vision Actionable

As we mentioned previously, vision statements work best when they are actionable. In this section, we provide three examples of how we have made our innovation vision actionable across our organization so that it is embedded in our day-to-day work.

Research and Development Day or Week

For the past two years, our course development and multimedia teams have been setting aside time to tackle challenges through brainstorming, tool development, and research into new technologies. Previous projects have included creating an augmented reality application, testing 3D images to work with a virtual reality headset, improving online course templates, and creating new faculty development resources. The instructional design team sets aside 1 day for this work; however, the multimedia team carves out a 30-hour week once per year with 5 to 6 hours of each workday devoted to research and design. This dedicated time has served not only to move teams forward in their innovations with courses and faculty but also as a motivational and team-building effort.

Additionally, team members use this time to cross-train one another on newer technologies or different ways of thinking about a problem. For example, an expert in user experience made a presentation to the multimedia team on color theory and graphic design principles. Instructional designers on the team also discuss their past experience working for other institutions as well as the insights they gained from their graduate work. Encouraging our staff to learn from each other is one way we are advancing innovation in our teams.

Innovation Team

Just as we asked our instructional design and multimedia teams to set aside specific times for innovation work, we have also created space and time for a team devoted to moving innovation projects forward for the entire online education organization. This team is composed of eight staff members from across the organization who applied to be members of the innovation team. Each member serves a one-year term so that others in the organization can also contribute to this team over time. The team chair serves a second year as a member at large to improve continuity from year to year. We believe that innovation is everyone's job and not just the work of a creative few. One of the jobs of team members is to vet innovation ideas from their colleagues and to serve as a kind of incubator for larger innovation explorations across the organization so that no good idea gets lost. The innovation team does not currently have its own budget aside from the staff time devoted to its projects, although as a large organization, discretionary funding is available for key projects. Even though this is a newer structure that we have implemented in the organization (a little more than one year old), this team formalizes our commitment to innovation in the long term.

Cross-Industry Professional Development

An additional way we encourage innovation across all our staff is to allow them to pursue professional development that crosses industries. For example, our research staff members attended a podcasting conference, and our multimedia team attends game developer conferences. Several members of our organization have attended strategy and training sessions on social media. These professional development opportunities allow our staff to have a broader vision of the field than what is currently happening in higher education, which, admittedly, is not always as speedy as in other industries. When our staff engage in professional development across industries, they obtain up-to-date knowledge of the latest trends and translate that knowledge into our higher education setting.

Allowing Your Vision to Mature

Although the key purposes of a vision discussed in the previous sections have been forefront in our minds for many years, a specific kind of innovation, disruptive innovation (Christensen, Raynor, & McDonald, 2015), is also pertinent to our discussion in this chapter. Although we certainly would not claim that we set out to achieve disruptive innovation intentionally, hindsight tells us that Oregon State University's Ecampus has experienced and, indeed, continues to experience many of the hallmarks of this theory of innovation. A disruptive innovator begins by serving an unserved or underserved portion of the market, "gaining a foothold by delivering more-suitable functionality—frequently at a lower price" (Christensen et al., 2015, p. 46). Once the foothold is established, the disruptive innovator then hones the quality of the product or service, often focusing on improving functionality or providing unique functionality. Ultimately, it catches on in the mainstream marketplace once quality reaches a high enough level. The incumbent then is either displaced or incorporates the disruption by "investing in sustaining innovations" (p. 50) and evolves.

Today, hindsight helps us understand our innovative journey through this theoretical lens. However, we did not set out to intentionally accomplish innovative disruption. The vision for innovation that launched Oregon State University's foray into online education was actually much more practical in nature and immediate in focus. As part of a land-grant institution, our start-up distance education unit needed to increase access to education for residents throughout the state, and to do this well, we needed revenue. That nascent vision is memorialized on a slip of paper, circa 2002, pinned to the current associate provost's office bulletin board. It reads:

1. Income potential
2. Alignment with institutional priorities
3. Investment of our resources
4. Long-term sustainability and benefit
5. Capacity to leverage external and internal resources

Clearly, with four out of five guidelines relating to resources, revenue generation was recognized as essential for launching our distance education initiative. These guidelines served as a decision-making framework—a vision to guide innovation, if not a vision for innovation itself.

Over a relatively short period, this vision matured. Another slip of paper pinned to the same bulletin board states our distance education unit's mission, circa 2004, and includes the following four tenets:

1. Offer compelling learning experiences that employ technology and non-traditional delivery methods to increase educational access anytime, anywhere.
2. Respond to the changing needs of lifelong learners by creating and delivering quality educational experiences.
3. Serve as the agent for institutional change by identifying and applying new technologies and models of teaching and learning to enable Oregon State University to lead in the increasingly competitive higher educational market.
4. Extend the resources of Oregon State University to the people of Oregon.

The vision underlying this mission statement stretches beyond start-up revenue generation; enunciates our values and constituencies; and, with references to technology, change, and growth, indicates a growing awareness that innovation was not only something we needed to get started but also something we needed for sustainability.

Yet another slip of paper on the bulletin board, circa 2010, finally embraced innovation as a core value, a strategy for meeting our institution's goals and our constituents' needs, and as part of our very identity:

Oregon State University Ecampus provides innovative and creative leadership to expand access to Oregon State University's academic excellence to diverse learners worldwide through the market-driven development and delivery of exceptional learning opportunities.

The irony of having a paper trail of our evolving vision for innovation in distance education is not lost on us. This tangible, humble reminder of our evolution as an organization provides us with a sense of our history, as well as a reminder of how innovation has always been at the heart of what we do.

Today, our vision for innovation is much clearer and top of mind. We recognize that innovation occasionally involves the invention of something wholly new, but as we found in our earliest days, we believe that more often innovation means creatively solving a problem or meeting a need. Moreover, we believe innovation means doing these things especially well, or at least better than before. We are not simply looking for other ways to bring an Oregon State University education to more learners, we are looking for better ways. We still believe that innovation requires resources, especially start-up funds when creating new organizations and initiatives, but we also believe that investments in innovation are needed for sustainability, such as for research and development, quality assurance, and management over the long haul. Experience has taught us that although innovation is often thrilling, it can also be isolating. Finally, we believe that innovation should be woven into strategic thinking and planning and is most powerful and impactful when it is aligned with the university's mission and goals.

Concluding Thoughts: Next Steps

As you think about your own vision for innovation on your campus, the following six steps may be helpful to get you started:

1. Review visions of other online education units, institutions, companies, and organizations. Looking at other organizations' vision statements can you give you some ideas about the range of what is being used. You may also want to focus on peer institutions or what you consider to be aspirational institutions.
2. Brainstorm about your audience and its needs. Knowing your audience's needs will be key to your vision statement. You will want to explore your regional audience but also think beyond your region where you may be able to share your signature areas with a broader audience.
3. Explore your institution's mission and vision. Your innovation vision should be aligned with your institution's mission and vision, and it may also offer the opportunity to expand what your institution is currently known for. This alignment can help prompt leadership across the institution to buy into the innovation.

4. Think about what you want your culture to look like. Consider your institution and your online learning organization 5 to 10 years from now. What does it look like? Who is it serving? What is it known for?

5. Refer to previous goals for guidance about future mission. If your online education organization has been functioning for quite some time without a vision for innovation, you may be able to look to your previous goals for inspiration. Where have you put your most time and energy in the past? What has helped you to be successful thus far?

6. Consider how your ideas for vision might affect your brand identity. Your brand identity is how your vision for innovation will be communicated to a broader audience. It will tell others what you want to be known for. Your brand identity on innovation may also influence the larger institutional brand identity.

References

Christensen, C. M., Raynor, M. E., & McDonald, R. (2015). What is disruptive innovation? *Harvard Business Review*. Retrieved from https://hbr.org/2015/12/what-is-disruptive-innovation

Oregon State University. (2017). *OSU strategic plan.* Retrieved from http://leadership.oregonstate.edu/strategicplan

Setser, B., & Morris, H. (2015). Building a culture of innovation in higher education: Design and practice for leaders. Retrieved from https://library.educause.edu/~/media/files/library/2015/4/ngt1502-pdf.pdf

3

INNOVATIVE
FINANCIAL MODELS

Rovy Branon, Lisa L. Templeton, Nelson C. Baker, and Kathryn E. Linder

llen, Seaman, Poulin, and Straut (2016) argue that "a continuing failure of online education has been the inability to convince its most important audience—higher education faculty members—of its worth" (p. 26). The skepticism from faculty toward online education is troubling for a number of reasons, particularly given the research legitimizing online education as equivalent to face-to-face and blended classrooms in terms of learning outcomes (McNamara, Swalm, Stearne, & Covassin, 2008; Odell, Abbitt, Amos, & Davis, 1999; Scoville & Buskirk, 2007; U.S. Department of Education, 2010). In addition to questioning the legitimacy of online education, faculty members also express concerns about the time and resources needed to design and teach online courses and may have little motivation to learn the skills needed to teach online, particularly later in their careers. In short, online education has, and continues to have, a public relations problem among faculty members.

One response to this skepticism as lack of motivation has been the generation of innovative financial models that may help incentivize faculty members and departments to try online courses and programs. Although distance education is not a new field, it can be a new initiative for faculty members or departments depending on their previous experiences with online education. As online units are combined with more traditional structures on campuses, it is important to think about different ways of incentivizing campus partners through innovative financial models.

Almost from the beginning, e-learning as an industry has been explored in terms of its revenue-generating power (see, e.g., Huynh, Umesh, & Valacich, 2003). However, more current literature on innovative financial models in distance education is limited. This may be, in part, because distance education programs are in such competition with one another for enrollments and national rankings that their administrators are unwilling to share information about their financial models. Although some research has been conducted on the revenue generation for online academic resources (Guthrie, Griffiths, & Maron, 2008) and massive open online courses (Hoxby, 2014; Kim, 2014), this chapter is one of the few contributions to the literature on financial models for online education programs that offers more detailed information and also includes institutional case studies.

This chapter offers an overview of several financial models and incentive structures including fee for service, revenue sharing, at-scale, and third-party integration, along with examples of each with details on their benefits and challenges.

Overview of Financial Models

George Box, the late statistician from the University of Wisconsin, once stated that "all models are wrong, but some are useful" (Box & Draper, 1987, p. 424). Financial models are no different; they all have benefits and drawbacks. It is a challenge to separate any model from the context in which it is intended to be used, but some underlying commonalities are a part of these models: management of financial risk, incentives, and revenue sharing.

Management of Financial Risk

All academic programs carry some measure of financial risk. Even when market research shows demand for a degree, there are always unknown factors. Risk comes from failing to generate enough enrollments from the outset or from changes in the market that result in sudden or long-term losses in enrollments. Some losses are expected at the start-up of a program, but shutting a program down is always an expensive endeavor. Risk is often masked for traditional programs at many universities because of the use of cross-subsidies to maintain a breadth of offerings. Although some online degree programs may operate with a similar centralized approach to risk, many are intended to generate net operating revenue (profit) for the university. This means that universities might choose to manage risk differently. In other words, a specific online degree program may be expected to be revenue neutral or return net revenue and must therefore maintain its own financial sustainability without a subsidy from other programs.

The management of financial risk is dependent on the type of financial models used by the university. Although it is beyond the scope of this chapter to explore university financial models in detail, it is helpful to understand some dynamics. The most basic characteristic of a university financial model is the degree to which revenue flow is centralized versus decentralized. Historically, universities used various forms of common area maintenance or black box budgeting, in which monies were centralized and then redistributed back to colleges and schools based on formulas, need, or just old-fashioned intuition (Policano, 2016). The complexity of university budgets, the demand for transparency, and the growing recognition that budgets are a significant way administration can incentivize change have driven changes to this approach.

More decentralized and transparent budget models have become more common in an attempt to deal with shrinking external subsidies (Policano, 2016). Decentralized models put more financial decision-making authority and accountability in the hands of deans and other unit-level leaders. Many varieties of responsibility center management have emerged that temper the highly localized approach; some control remains with central administration but the majority of responsibility is placed with local units.

The management of financial risk varies greatly between the two extreme approaches. As might be expected, financial losses or net revenues are often managed or maintained by the administration in common area maintenance universities, whereas colleges, schools, or even departments are expected to manage financial risk in responsibility center management universities. Although online learning provides the potential for financial growth, the management of financial risk is one element that should be decided before moving forward. The following are some basic risk areas that a model should cover.

Upfront Production and Development Costs
Online programs generally require more upfront expenses in the form of instructional design, video production, and technical development. Additionally, marketing costs can be higher than they are for traditional programs if the intent is to reach students outside areas typically served by the university.

Annualized Losses
Every program faces the possibility of temporary declines in enrollment. Online programs that start with high enrollment expectations and set budgets accordingly are riskier than programs that are intended to start small and grow. Even mature programs can face new competition or declines because of temporary or permanent shifts in the market. If an online program is expected to generate and sustain itself through tuition revenue, deciding whether losses from temporary enrollment declines will be absorbed by a

central unit, school, or college, or rolled forward as a program deficit should come before launching.

Costs to Sunset a Program

Closing or sunsetting a program is always a difficult decision. A program sunset often results when losses are realized; for some programs, it is the first time a true reckoning occurs. Assuming losses are held at the program level, any deficits that have rolled forward will need to be covered and all teach out costs will also need to be considered. Depending on the size of the program, number of courses, and whether the program follows predictable rigid cohorts or has a more flexible schedule, the costs can be considerable. Like the determination of risk management for annual losses, decisions about how a program sunset will be paid for should be determined before starting a program, not after it is in trouble.

Incentives

Beyond risk management, any financial model will incentivize certain behaviors and disincentivize others. In cases where the specific incentives are not explicitly explained, they often emerge after the model is running and imbalances start to occur. For example, if the goal is to incentivize programs with high numbers of enrollments, then revenue-share models may be more effective than fee-for-service models (more on these models later in the chapter). Models may periodically need to be reexamined if the types of program development do not reflect the intent or mission of the university. How revenue is shared or flows is a significant element of how a given model incentivizes behaviors.

Revenue Sharing or Flows

The flow of revenue at any university is complex. Many costs are not easily captured as direct charges, there is rarely the upfront money to invest in online program development and marketing, and there are always competing demands for any net revenue (i.e., profits). Some of the revenue flows that must be considered include university overhead, department revenue, online production unit costs, and other requirements for sharing revenue with central administration.

Overhead Costs

Overhead costs are generally simple to calculate and are often the same across university programming. Sometimes called indirect costs, overhead costs cover the necessary costs of running the university that are often not direct costs for running a program. Everything from information technology to building maintenance to the cost of administration salaries is often included in overhead. One early decision when developing a new financial model is to determine whether university overhead will be included as a part of the financial model or be taken after all revenues are distributed.

Flows to Departments, Schools, and Colleges

One component that will differ by university, and in some cases even by each college or school, is how much revenue will be captured at each level. Will departments or those running the program retain any revenue? Will it be captured at the college or school level or returned to the central online unit? There is no one correct answer to these questions, but as Policano (2016) notes, universities are leaning toward higher local control and responsibility for funding decisions.

Flows to the Online Units

Online production and marketing are often far more expensive than the typical direct costs for running university programs. All stakeholders need to understand the costs of high-quality instructional design and the differences when marketing to students who can find and attend a competing online program with one click. Depending on how these costs are structured, who owns the risk, and the length of time to pay back upfront expenses, the online unit will need more direct revenue than departments typically spend on traditional, face-to-face programs. The costs to run the online unit, including ongoing investments in future technology, can be a source of contention if not fully understood and agreed on at the outset.

Flows to the Center of the Institution

Finally, in addition to university overhead, some online programs are also expected to return additional net revenue to the university coffers. In some cases, the expected amount of net revenue to the university increases each year, creating an expectation of consistent growth. Although such expectations can incentivize program growth, there should be clarity about what happens when there is a market change or other factors that reduce enrollments.

Faculty compensation. Faculty compensation is the majority of the core expense for any university degree program, and online programs are no different. The way faculty are compensated is an important consideration for any model. Some models budget actual faculty salary as a direct expense. If the most senior department faculty are developing and teaching in the online program, then costs will be higher. A direct expense approach offers the flexibility to use more senior faculty and works better with high-salary departments. In other models, departments are given a fixed course buyout fee that splits the difference between senior, junior, and adjunct faculty. Fixed faculty buyout costs are easier to budget and puts some responsibility in the hands of the department to manage the faculty mix. A disadvantage to a fixed approach is that departments with highly compensated faculty may not be able to work within a standard budget.

Investments. Ongoing investments are required for online learning just like they are for face-to-face learning. The difference is that these costs are not likely to have the same interest from donors or state legislators. It is much easier to have someone pay for a new building (possibly with their name on it) than to invest in the latest learning management system or video production studio tools. Yet these and other investments are just as critical to maintaining a quality teaching environment as a new roof or heating system is for physical classrooms. These systems require people with sophisticated instructional design, media production, and, increasingly, evaluation and data analytics knowledge. The cost is not only systems but also the human infrastructure needed.

In addition to teaching and learning investments, marketing systems are also critical to the modern online learning enterprise. A customer relationship management system is a minimal requirement, but increasingly sophisticated marketing automation and analytics tools are essential for scalable operations. New approaches and investments will be needed as marketing becomes more advanced. Marketing teams that began as public relations and communications can require significant changes in management and expenses to become a data-driven marketing team. Similar to the advances in teaching and learning, marketing investments should also include the expense of specialized human resources.

In the remainder of this chapter, we offer an overview of four financial models that are particular to online education organizations: fee-for-service, revenue share, at-scale, and revenue share with a third-party organization. In addition to describing each model, we also review potential pros and cons associated with each.

Fee-for-Service Models

Fee-for-service models in a university often involve an internal unit charging direct costs for services needed to run an online program. These services typically include instructional design, production support, marketing, and other administrative services. A simple fee-for-service model uses hourly rates to charge actual service time to a program. The cost of an instructional designer, for example, is billed to a department for the actual hours worked. Billing can be for fixed services (i.e., the cost to build a single course is $50,000) or it might be based on billable hours.

Simple fee-for-service models have an advantage of being transparent and clear. Each service cost is itemized, and all parties can see how much is spent on a given service. The waters begin to muddy a bit when you start to account for overhead and other costs that must be included in the hourly rates or service charges. These costs, however, are generally easy enough to break down and show to all stakeholders. Another advantage of fee-for-service models is that once the expenses are covered, the academic unit retains all revenue. Retaining all revenue after expenses can be a significant incentive for departments and faculty to develop online programs.

The required investments and financial risk of online degree programs are challenging to cover using a traditional fee-for-service model. Universities are increasingly moving toward more complex fee-for-service arrangements or revenue-share models for flexibility. (Revenue-share models are covered following this section.)

Types of Service Fees

Fee-for-service models begin by establishing rates for certain types of services, which may include instructional design, video production, other multimedia development (e.g., animations, graphics, educational games, interactive elements, etc.), service or maintenance fees, and other overhead charges. Some universities structure these fees as bundles with a fixed cost. For example, a fee for designing and developing an online course may include all activities, including media production in a single fixed fee. Other universities charge hourly rates for each of these services. The more granular the fee structure, the more flexible and easy it is to customize, but each service charge adds more complexity to projects and becomes a challenge to manage and explain to campus partners.

Some fees are charged per program or per course; generally, the online unit charges the academic unit offering the degree. These fees can include online design, administration, and marketing costs, but in some cases those fees are broken down and charged separately (see the University of Washington model in Box 3.1).

Risk or Opportunity Management

Simple fee-for-service models do not address financial risk related to program failure. The online unit generally provides a set of services paid for by the academic unit or from a central fund. The management of financial risk in fee-for-service models typically falls under the mechanisms used to underwrite risk for other programs unless specified. The University of Washington model (Box 3.1) shows one way risk management can be handled in a fee-for-service model.

Overhead and Central Costs

In fee-for-service models, university indirect costs are sometimes included in pricing but are often handled directly between the academic unit and central administration. This approach can be simple but should be clarified at the outset. Online unit administrators should determine whether they must also pay overheads on the internal service fees or if such overheads are double dipping. In other words, if the academic unit pays overhead costs once when students pay for a program, then paying overhead costs again for internal charges through the online unit might be considered taxing the same money twice.

Benefits and Drawbacks

This model offers very high local control over service decisions. Faculty or program leaders can choose which services to purchase to support their programs, which can maximize financial returns to the unit. Unless modified, like the University of Washington model (see Box 3.1), investment in new programs and risk management must be explicitly handled through central administration or by the unit. This model also assumes that academic departments know what services are needed to adequately support a quality online program, and that may not always be the case.

Because the online education market is still relatively new and changing rapidly, fee-for-service models are challenging to keep functional at scale. Revenue-share models are increasingly common as the need for ongoing investment, management of risk, and relative simplicity are needed. The next section discusses several different revenue-share models, followed by a discussion of at-scale models revenue sharing with third-party online program management companies.

Revenue-Share Models

One way to incentivize faculty, departments, and colleges is through a revenue-share model that creates a win-win situation for the online education unit and the academics units that are contributing to the online courses and programs. In a revenue-share model, a percentage of the funding from the tuition generated from online courses or programs is sent directly to the

BOX 3.1
University of Washington Fixed Fee-Based Model

The University of Washington began running self-sustaining degree programs more than 30 years ago. These programs are administered through a unit called Continuum College, which also manages a range of other continuing education activities. Continuum College makes upfront investments in degree programs, manages self-sustaining program financial risk, and provides services (marketing, registration, financial management, etc.) to the academic schools and colleges that grant the degrees. Over 20 years, the model has launched more than 108 programs and more than 99% are still running. Fifteen of the 108 programs are fully online.

The University of Washington approach puts nearly all financial decision-making authority in the hands of the department, whereas risk and shared services are managed through the university's Continuum College.

Three primary fees are charged: A fixed fee per program, a fixed fee per course, and a risk/opportunity fee that starts at 6% of gross degree revenue and declines 1% each year after a program breaks even until it reaches zero. This risk model means that older more predictable programs pay substantially less than newer unproven programs, and the academic unit retains the additional net revenue. This approach incentivizes program leaders to break even as early as possible so they can capture more revenue.

When a program starts, Continuum College provides all the start-up funds for the program, including faculty costs, and holds all of the risk. Departments manage and keep all revenue beyond the fees, which they must pay (i.e., this is not an à la carte approach; all fees are required). Total charge costs, including central university overhead, average 22% of gross degree revenue, but older programs pay as little as 15% of gross revenue because of the declining risk charge.

Although this model was created before online delivery was common, its flexibility has worked well for hybrid and online programs. One addition to accommodate online program cost is the addition of service charges for instructional design and video production. These charges are also fixed fees and are charged on a per course basis. The success of this fixed-fee approach means that the model will continue to be used for self-sustaining online programs at the University of Washington for the foreseeable future.

department or college that is creating the online course or program. These funds can then be used for additional growth of online courses or programs, faculty development related to online teaching and learning, or individualized faculty incentives such as course buyouts to create time for the development of new online courses and programs.

Because online education can require additional skills and time on the part of the faculty members teaching the courses, incentives for online teaching are important. Online course creation and facilitation are not easy tasks and should be incentivized, especially for beginning instructors. For faculty members and departments who are concerned about a lack of time or resources to create and teach online courses, the revenue-share model can act as a problem-solving mechanism by contributing additional resources to help alleviate these burdens. Revenue sharing can help create the time and support needed for everyone involved to engage in creating online courses and programs.

Moreover, online courses are often not a part of faculty members' position descriptions. Perhaps most important, many universities are still working on integrating online teaching into promotion and tenure documentation. Each of these reasons—the extra time and skills, the overload work, and the risk of doing online teaching without official recognition—create the need to incentivize the work.

Revenue sharing is often a completely new idea for departments and colleges. Although the integration of a revenue-share model depends on the university budget model, it is usually uncommon for credit hours to be connected to a department or college's funding model. However, the benefits of a revenue-share model are clear: Faculty members and departments can see an immediate financial gain for the work they put into the development of quality online courses and programs, promoting those courses and programs, and scaling their online offerings to attract more and diverse student populations. Revenue-share models also create natural pathways for scaling online courses and programs when the funding is reinvested in the online education mission of the department.

Typically, revenue sharing can create two kinds of incentives. The first is through course and program development stipends and faculty buyouts that give faculty members more time to develop online courses and programs. This kind of incentive can be funded at the department level or through the central administration of online education. The second incentive is funding to support the delivery of teaching. This kind of incentive might fund overloads for faculty, pay for the cost of instruction for online courses or programs, or create the possibility of increased faculty development initiatives or programs.

Despite these benefits, there are some challenges with the revenue-share model—for example, getting it started. Launching new online courses or programs requires funding up front, and a scarcity of resources and time can cause challenges to generating an initial series of online courses or a program that will eventually generate revenue. There are also additional difficulties with sharing revenue when a program is initially launched and money is tight. It is important to also revisit revenue-share models over time (see Box 3.2) to make sure they still fit the scale and needs of a department.

Depending on institutional cultures, some universities might need more incentives than others to attract faculty and departments to create online courses and programs. There are several different kinds of revenue-share models, and they each have their benefits and challenges.

BOX 3.2

**Example of a Revenue Model Scaling Over Time at
Oregon State University**

When Ecampus was first developed at Oregon State University, it was launched using a Fund for the Improvement of Postsecondary Education grant. That seed funding allowed an 80–20 tuition revenue share between each college that was launching online courses and programs (80%) and the administration of those programs through Ecampus (20% to fund student support services, marketing of courses, online course development assistance, etc.). A distance education fee was also charged to fund Ecampus operations.

Over time, as Ecampus revenue grew, that tuition revenue-sharing model was shifted to include some funds being sent to the central administration of the university in a 80–10–10 model in which colleges still received 80% of revenue, and the central administration and Ecampus administration each received 10%.

This model shifted again with Ecampus being fully funded with the student fee and the colleges receiving 80% of revenue and the central administration of the university receiving 20% of revenue. In the current model Ecampus is funded as a line item in the overall university budget. As the revenue for Ecampus grew over time, the revenue-sharing model shifted to accommodate the different needs for growth and incentives across the university.

Model 1: Percentage of Tuition

In this revenue-share model, different stakeholders at the university share the tuition generated through online programs. Each stakeholder group receives a percentage of the revenue that is generated through the online tuition.

- Benefits: This kind of model helps to scale online initiatives as courses and programs grow and create additional revenue for everyone at the table.
- Challenges: Because this model depends on tuition, courses and programs need to be marketed well and have consistent enrollments for this revenue-share model to scale and grow. Also, negotiating the percentages each stakeholder receives can involve difficult conversations. The percentages may also need to be revisited on a regular basis and renegotiated as programs scale up or down and create more revenue, or as new stakeholders or campus partners become involved in online course and program creation.

Model 2: Technology or Student Services Fee

In this revenue-share model, a student fee is used to create the revenue that is shared across stakeholder groups. This model can be combined with the percentage-of-tuition model described previously to create a larger funding pot to scale up and expand online initiatives.

- Benefits: For large-scale online programs, this kind of model can create a consistent budget for administering campuswide support of online education across departments.
- Challenges: Student fees may not rise over time, so this model depends on the increased enrollment of new students to generate additional revenue.

Model 3: Head Count or Credit Hour

In this revenue-share model, student head counts in online courses or programs or the credit hours taught by various departments are used to decide how much revenue should be shared with different stakeholder groups.

- Benefits: This model encourages equity across groups, especially if certain departments have larger online programs than others. This model can also incentivize departments to increase their enrollments and online offerings to increase their revenue share.

- Challenges: Departments with smaller online offerings may not be incentivized enough to market their online courses and programs or scale and grow their offerings.

At-Scale Models

At-scale models use a combination of market research and enrollment projections over time to determine the cost structures of a program as it scales up or down (see Box 3.3 for an example of an at-scale model). At-scale models explore direct, variable, and indirect costs, and costs for third-party services and technologies. Direct costs are fixed for the program and do not vary based on enrollment, whereas variable costs depend on enrollments. Overhead costs, or indirect costs, include activities (often administrative) not directly tied to the academic mission. In each of these categories, third-party costs might emerge to support the needs of the organization.

Using these four cost categories, an organization can create a cost structure based on enrollment scenarios. In other words, the organization can predict how many enrollments are needed to cover costs and at what point it might break even, and, ultimately, decide the level of the risk university administrators might be willing to undertake. These calculations can then be used to set a tuition price that ensures that all costs are covered.

Using an at-scale model, it becomes incredibly important to track revenues and expenses. The organization needs an early-warning system to identify potential risks in deficit spending. These same systems ensure that predictions are being realized and that midstream corrections can be made if needed. Also, in the creation and operation of programs at scale, new characteristics for assessing risk and compliance must be part of the university decision-making, including personnel who leave the university, compliance, and return on investment.

Personnel Who Leave the University

Determining the financial, legal (intellectual property), and social considerations for faculty who have created a course and then leave employment at the university are interesting new wrinkles in budget models. When deciding to develop a course that should last three years, do you redevelop the course for new faculty in such transitions?

Compliance

From state authorization, to regional- and program-level accreditation, each regulatory consideration takes on slightly new tones based on the scale of the program, the number of students in a section, and how faculty and the university provide evidence of quality and student engagement.

BOX 3.3
Georgia Tech At-Scale Model Example

When Georgia Tech launched its massive open online course initiative, several questions emerged. Could quality be maintained while reaching more individuals? Could the cost of the degree be reduced through a different cost structure? In a methodical process, a Georgia Tech team began to look at the various factors that contribute to cost structures and enrollments to create a new business model for higher education and quality programs built on rigor and scale at a very different price point.

Administrators of universities, especially public universities, often face challenges in managing cash flows for large investments across fiscal year boundaries. This program was no different. The enrollment projections compared to the cost requirements showed that it would take three years before the university would have sufficient tuition revenue to pay for the ongoing costs. Further, there were sizable start-up costs in creating the curricular materials before any enrollments would take place.

With this knowledge, university officials set out to determine if other sources would find this endeavor compelling enough to underwrite the initial start-up costs. Could the initial costs be offset through the philanthropic activities of either corporate or individual contributions? Would an entity come forward that could not only believe the organizers would be successful but also help tell a story about how higher education can be and is innovating to meet the needs of learners?

Georgia Tech was deeply appreciative of the response from AT&T to this request. AT&T's foundation was most generous and supportive, providing an initial gift of $2 million and ultimately a second gift, which kept the program from ever being cash negative. AT&T management saw the program as changing the landscape of higher education and wanted to help foster a change for all higher education while also enabling workers in the technology sector to benefit from the knowledge of the computer science master's degree program.

Return on Investment

Institution leaders must also consider their return on investment while staying competitive with features needed for a new program. With the technology landscape for educational products rapidly growing in terms of new feature sets and new entrants, a university must make the investments needed to operate at scale while simultaneously seeking sufficient revenues to pay for new technologies and tools. One strategy is through forming partnerships with third-party organizations, discussed in the following section.

Revenue Sharing With Third-Party Organizations

Every university approaches online learning from a different starting point. In some cases, mature continuing education, academic technology support, and other core infrastructures needed to build and sustain online learning already exist. In those cases, the models described previously provide different ways to approach sharing within an institution.

As the famous fiction author William Gibson (1999) once said in an interview, "The future is here—it's just not very evenly distributed." For institutions that have not created the infrastructure or do not have the funding to finance the start-up of online programs, a number of third-party companies now exist to provide these services. These companies go by different names, but the common term is *online program manager* (OPM). Many, but not all, of these companies use a variant on the percentage of tuition model described earlier in this chapter. Although many of the contracts between universities and OPMs are not public, published articles show that they require as much as 50% of gross tuition revenue with more than 10-year required terms (Lieberman, 2017).

Financial Benefits

The most significant financial benefit to working with an OPM is that the university can avoid the very high upfront investment costs in learning technology, instructional design, and marketing. OPMs can amortize ongoing platform and personnel investments across multiple universities. This can lower their overall operating costs, and those savings might be passed along to the university, or they can add to the OPM profit margin. In some cases, the OPMs also own the financial risk for any start-up costs or program failure.

OPMs also bring a substantial working knowledge and often have deep expertise in marketing and instructional design. This knowledge is further enhanced by their familiarity with best practices across multiple universities. As was previously mentioned, the need to consider human resource infrastructure is key to financial sustainability.

Caveats and Considerations

The long payback period and high revenue share can help universities move into online offerings faster and with lower risk. The caveat, of course, is that the long contract times create a very profitable business model for the OPM. That profit is also money that the university could use to further its mission, develop its own capabilities, or fill other revenue shortfalls. One recommendation is for universities to conduct a long-term return-on-investment analysis to see whether the high revenue share is worth it over time. The return on investment should take into account not just 1 or 2 programs but the total growth in online programs the university would like to see over a 10-year period. The lost dollars can be quite staggering when such growth is factored into the equation.

Investment costs that initially seem unreachable can look much more reasonable over time when 20% to 30% of gross revenue can cover operational costs from an internal unit versus up to 50% for an external company. In the event that no capital exists to start an online program, another recommendation is to begin using some shared revenue to build up university capabilities. This is difficult because much of that revenue might be used to cover operational expenses, but it helps to build a long-term investment amount into the base budget.

In any case, a strong exit strategy should be written into any contract that takes into account data and course interoperability (be sure there is an agreement that all courses will work in the university learning management system in the event of a separation), student information (including all customer relationship management records), and all prospective student data (marketing leads).

The OPM market is changing rapidly, and new models are emerging that recognize the limitations of external revenue sharing (Hill, 2016). Unbundled services are disrupting the once disruptive OPM market, and competition is beginning to drive better revenue-share deals or enhanced fee-for-service offerings. As the rapid pace of change continues, higher education leaders are encouraged to follow financial management trends at other institutions and at the companies that support online education.

As several chapters in this volume illustrate, having funds to try new things and incentivize new projects is critical. Although online teaching and learning continue to grow and change, online organizations need to be nimble and innovative with their revenue models. Funds brought in through online organizations are often used to support the institution and to expand programs, but they are also needed to support innovative endeavors. Traditional university budget models do not always have the flexibility to dedicate funds to explore alternative and new areas of growth. This is where online education has provided a model for innovation and potential revenue generation, often in more traditional academic environments.

References

Allen, I. E., Seaman, J., Poulin, R., & Straut, T. T. (2016). *Online report card: Tracking online education in the United States.* Babson Park, MA: Babson Survey Research Group and Quahog Research Group.

Box, G. E. P., & Draper, N. R. (1987). *Empirical model building and response surfaces.* New York, NY: Wiley.

Gibson, W. (1999, November 30). The science of science fiction. Interview by B. Gladstone. *Talk of the Nation* [Radio broadcast]. Washington DC: National Public Radio.

Guthrie, K., Griffiths, R., & Maron, N. (2008). *Sustainability and revenue models for online academic resources: An Ithaka report.* Retrieved from https://sca.jiscinvolve.org/wp/files/2008/06/sca_ithaka_sustainability_report-final.pdf

Hill, P. (2016, September 8). Online program management: An updated view of the market landscape [Web log post]. Retrieved from https://mfeldstein.com/online-program-management-updated-view-market-landscape/

Hoxby, C. M. (2014). The economics of online postsecondary education: MOOCs, nonselective education, and highly selective education. *American Economic Review, 104,* 528–533.

Huynh, M. Q., Umesh, U. N., & Valacich, J. S. (2003). E-learning as an emerging entrepreneurial enterprise in universities and firms. *Communications of the Association for Information Systems, 12*(3), 48–68.

Kim, P. (Ed.). (2014). *Massive open online courses: The MOOC revolution.* New York, NY: Routledge.

Lieberman, M. (2017, October 25). Competing models among OPM providers. *Inside Higher Ed.* Retrieved from https://www.insidehighered.com/digital-learning/article/2017/10/25/opms-fee-service-growing-revenue-share-models-dominate

McNamara, J. M., Swalm, R. L., Stearne, D. J., & Covassin, T. M. (2008). Online weight training. *Journal of Strength and Conditioning Research, 22,* 1164–1168.

Odell, M., Abbitt, J., Amos, D., & Davis, J. (1999). Developing online courses: A comparison of Web-based instruction with traditional instruction. In J. Price et al. (Eds.), *Proceedings of Society for Information Technology & Teacher Education International Conference 1999* (pp. 126–130). Chesapeake, VA: Association for the Advancement of Computing in Education.

Policano, A. J. (2016). *From ivory tower to glass house: Strategies for academic leaders during turbulent times.* Irvine, CA: Zepoli.

Scoville, S. A., & Buskirk, T. D. (2007). Traditional and virtual microscopy compared experimentally in a classroom setting. *Clinical Anatomy, 20,* 565–570.

U.S. Department of Education. (2010). *Evaluation of evidence-based practices in online learning: A meta-analysis and review of online learning studies.* Washington, DC: Author.

4

INNOVATION VIA CONSORTIUM

Brad Wheeler, James Hilton, Lois Brooks, and Dave King

Higher education in its 300-year evolution has at various times focused on the need to establish a single brand for each institution. The disaggregated brand-driven approach made sense in a highly distributed nondigital world, but it makes much less sense in a networked world where scale and aggregation drive economies. This chapter is the record of a conversation among Brad Wheeler, vice president and chief information officer at Indiana University; James Hilton, vice provost and dean of libraries at University of Michigan; Lois Brooks, vice provost and chief information officer at University of Wisconsin Madison; and Dave King, professor emeritus at Oregon State University. Wheeler, Hilton, and Brooks have been involved in consortium development over the years; most notably, with the establishment of the Sakai learning management system organization. All 4 contributors have been recognized for creative and innovative work in higher education across multiple decades and currently are deeply involved in the start-up consortium Unizin, a group of 11 major public universities and 2 university systems focusing on learner success. Unizin's mission is to improve the learner experience with technology-based teaching and learning resources with a focus on learner analytics.

Throughout the conversation, the contributors discuss the challenges of starting a consortium, the roles that consortia can play in innovation in the education technology space, and the value of consortia for institutions of higher education.

Dave: You all have histories with collaborative development—Sakai, HathiTrust, Kuali—all large scale education-based cooperatives.

Based on your experience, why now? Why is the world in need of more collaborative, consortium-based work now than it might have in the past?

Brad: I'll lead off with one comment, and that is, so many things that we are doing are deeply tech rich, and when I say *tech rich* I also mean the skills around them: licensing, buying things, aggregating things. Information technology is one of the native factors of economy of scale. When you do more information technology and grow in some size, unit costs decrease with volume. That is why you see so many large companies that are dominating their field. Or when six companies in a particular area buy each other up because the economies of scale, the flat, raw economics, I think are so compelling.

I think that is one of the factors. If there was no gain to the cost of a consortium, over doing everything yourself, just purely from a cost basis, where you had enough data on your own, then you would not do it. Creating a consortium takes considerable time, effort, and funding. If you don't gain the economy of scale from the consortium there would be no gain to creating the consortium. You put together these aggregations to try to access greater and greater economies of scale and of course, larger and larger data sets.

Lois: I think there's an acceleration component to this as well. What we are being tasked to do with technologies, as you said, is incredibly complex. Each of us developing these capabilities and services alone takes a long time to figure out the best approaches and get the work done. Our universities can't wait for us to spend a few years figuring out an interesting technical approach to solve an immediate, compelling problem. We need to be much more agile and responsive than we've been in the past. The collective work allows us to accelerate.

James: I like that as a theory, but I'm not convinced, based on the experiences I have had with consortia, that they accelerate you. They may bring you to a better solution, but I certainly don't usually experience it as acceleration. Unizin was 18 months in the incubation period before we could even get more than 3 or 4 institutions to engage in a serious way. For me the thing that drives the consortium approach is that the challenges facing higher education right now are bigger than any single institution. Our institutions have a history of competing with each other to our detriment and on the wrong dimensions.

In fact, we have been sold a whole bunch of solutions that are alleged to increase our competitive advantage. You have got to have new enterprise resource planning from PeopleSoft or Oracle or whatever, because that is going to give you better business intelligence, and you will be more competitive in your market. I think that logic is fundamentally flawed as it applies to higher ed. For the most part, we compete based on the quality of our students, our faculty, and our staff. The rest is just infrastructure. We have been pursuing infrastructure as though it gave you a competitive advantage. If it does not, let's pursue infrastructure as a consortium and take advantage of the economies of scale that Brad was talking about.

Even more disturbing than buying into the illusion of competitive advantage through infrastructure is that our tendency to see ourselves as individual islands in competition with each other has led to a situation where we now have to buy all our discoveries, publications, and data back from the aggregators. We are so focused on individual institution competition, that we sign deals with publishers, we sign deals with whomever, in hopes of getting better visibility and getting ourselves out front faster. The long-term consequence of acting independently is that we allow the market to aggregate our demand and dictate the terms to us for data content and discoveries that begin with us.

If we were still in a growth era for higher education, if the revenue trajectories for higher education were going up and up and up, that is all tolerable. That is not what the trajectory is right now. I think we have to find ways to, again, differentiate on the things that we actually care about and consolidate on places where there are economies of scale and economies and benefits of shared terms and understanding.

Dave: We have been in the digital environment for multiple years, actually multiple decades. Is the digital world a place where this is even more important for us than maybe it was when we were trying to work together in a predigital environment?

Brad: Absolutely, because in a predigital environment, the economies of scale are X, I think in a digital environment, they are X with an exponent. I literally mean that in the economics of it. Over time, there is some value in owning our own printing presses and producing numbers of books and such, but the economics of that don't scale in any way as they do when you're producing digital products, digital distribution, digital data.

From a pure economic lens, to mention a little bit of what James has touched on, I think there is also a great ecology of knowledge and information that grows when we do things together versus when we try to do them independently at each of our institutions. It has been difficult to translate that into acceleration. You would also have to gauge acceleration from where you are in the thought cycle. I think, in some cases, we were relatively early for aggregation.

James and I felt some frustration with how long it took to band together, get focused, enrolled, embodied, and then funded. If you were an institution whose administrators really had not given much thought to that at all—take our good friends in Nebraska, who came in a little bit later—by the time they turned their eyes to it, Unizin looked like a big accelerator because they just started thinking about it and that there's a way to go faster with their approach to technology-based teaching.

Lois: I would agree, and I also think the accelerator perspective is interesting because it depends on how much you're able to resource locally.

Dave: Just playing off what Lois just said, is this concept, the idea of going together farther. Does it work well in other places, or is the university environment relatively unique?

Brad: In universities, we have a culture we can share with each other when we choose to do so. However, we need to understand who actually makes a difference. In the past, we have tried to differentiate ourselves in ways that were not our faculty or our students or our degree programs—our true differentiators. We all got sold these digital teaching platforms and digital infrastructure one at a time. You all know. I have become seriously disillusioned with the learning environment, the learning management system [LMS] space.

What we learned in the 15 years since starting Sakai is when something like an LMS made a difference in faculty preference; if it even happened, it lasted only as long as that faculty member was at an institution. I doubt there was ever a faculty member in the world who wouldn't take a career opportunity to switch institutions and worried if the other institution ran Desire2Learn, or Blackboard, or whatever. We frittered away so much energy and so much effort over 15 years with nothing to show for it based on differentiating in that space.

I do think, particularly as we go to the cloud-scale era, that we should not make that mistake again. Let's aggregate. Let's cooperate, let's don't try to compete or differentiate on something that doesn't matter.

Lois: That is an interesting thread in here, but there is a different and additional spin on this, and that is that each of our universities do need to compete successfully in the marketplace. We need to be able to attract undergraduate and graduate students. The work we're doing allows us to be successful in that way. But I believe the university marketplace is going to consolidate. There will be colleges going out of business, and I wonder if these steps that we're taking now through this consortium work, and the scale economies, are a way to guard against that threat of failure.

Brad: I do not know if they protect us from the coming years when the student population is projected to decline substantially (which may drive some universities and colleges to go out of business). I think it is the core elements: the brand, the students, the faculty, and so forth, but they certainly should help with our ability to collectively learn and the economies and the cost of doing things that matter to the stability of an institution. Whether that is enough to differentiate or not, I am not sure. The coming student population declines are going to take out the weakest of the herd first. We could see a shakeout of 20% over the next 10 years.

James: I think that for me, there is a huge opportunity to get institutional differentiation right. If we can quit focusing on differentiating from each other on things that do not make any difference, we'll have a lot more energy to differentiate on the things that do make a difference. Again, it is always stunning to me when I watch provosts and presidents and vice presidents for research get together and put their game faces on. Collaboration is too often left outside the meeting room doors. Instead, they are focused on competition. At lead institutions, for example, individual administrators of universities are worried about whether they're climbing or falling in the latest rankings (e.g., Are they moving from 15 to 17 or vice versa?). It is completely understandable. Their boards are focused on those metrics, and everybody is behaving rationally. The problem is, we are at a moment when most of the country doesn't even realize why we have research universities. That's where I'm much more concerned about needing to differentiate to make the value proposition for institutions. We need a differentiated approach to education, not just a one-size-fits-all factory.

My observation is that our institution administrators tend to focus too much on things that they think will give them competitive advantage while ignoring the lack of differentiation in our messaging about the means and purposes of higher education. It is as if we all believed that if we did not have a killer LMS, we might lose students. If your school is one of the at-risk 20%

of institutions, maybe. But I will tell you nobody is coming to Michigan because of our LMS, and we need to focus on telling the story and demonstrating why public research universities matter to society.

Lois: I was thinking about it a little differently actually. I think the differentiator is the analytics that come out of this that allow you to tune your programs to compete.

Brad: I think that's really an important point. Again, from the business school perspective on this term *strategy*, even though it is fairly precise, it's used pretty loosely a lot. The terms *competitive advantage* and *comparative advantage* also have precise meanings. I do not think those of us in higher education in general have much sophistication at all in even understanding what competitive advantage means, but we use the words a lot.

Dave: I would agree with that too; that is why I was kind of pushing on whether universities have a unique need or expectation to become more collaborative and consortial, just because we don't understand the real competitive nature of what is going on in the world around us in many cases. In the mid-1990s, we were talking about there being 20 land-grant universities in 2020, down from the 67 there are now. Of course, none of that has happened, but I do think that these kinds of consortial efforts are based on trying to figure out not who's going to be the one falling out the bottom but who will be the ones who actually guide the way and lead at the top.

That is why when we talk about Unizin, I find it very compelling that we have founding members who are like-minded and can in fact pull together in a relatively singular direction to establish and meet goals that perhaps others will follow later. I think we're trying to create a competitive advantage even though some do not recognize the competitive environment we are in.

Brad: I think that is a fruitful line of thought. Some of you may have picked up Peter Senge's (2006) book on the learning organization. It really, and boldly, makes the point that the only enduring competitive advantage is learning how to learn faster than your rivals.

When we speak of learning how to learn faster, to improve our pedagogy in the classroom, to rethink and understand how students actually learn, we can then use that insight to shift our core sequences, to understand more deeply what distributed learning does versus residential learning and how to blend them together. That is the alchemy that, as you say, Dave, enlightens the front of the herd rather than debating about whether you're strong enough to not be at the back of the herd.

Lois: This might be a good segue into the question of how you would describe an effective consortium.

Brad: The process gains exceed process losses. When you aggregate people in a group meeting, you hope productivity would scale at least linearly if not exponentially. All the things we are gaining value from, whether it is the cost of software, or learning or sharing larger data, or whatever—all the gains must exceed the losses.

James: I agree with that 100%. I think that at some level, the key to a really good consortium, and the biggest challenge, is maintaining alignment of purpose. Even when I look at the institutions that have come into Unizin, the biggest challenge has been in making sure we continue to build alignment. Brad and I have talked about what led to the decline of institutional support for Sakai development. Part of what happened was the consortium lost alignment between the people who were making funding decisions and the people who were making product and road map decisions.

Dave: How do you avoid that? Is that a matter of taking your eye off the ball at some point, or is it a common evolution that probably is just going to happen over a period of time?

James: I definitely think it is a challenge. I think it is a challenge that faces consortia in a way that I am sure companies face as well, but companies have hierarchical tools to dictate vision and focus. The power we have is the power of rhetoric—the power of talking about what it is we are trying to do and where the shared vision is. Again, I think in any consortium you see tensions around all that. For example, you see tensions between how much time the leaders of the consortium should spend talking about direction and how much time should they spend talking about just doing things. You see that in our Unizin board meetings.

Dave: Let me shift gears a little bit here to get a little more specific focus on Unizin. Brad and James, you have both said that the Unizin consortium is designed to be the Internet2—the collaborative high-speed networking initiative founded by higher education—of online learning. What do you mean by that?

Brad: Just as those in higher ed realized connectivity was very important to enable research in the mid-to-late 1990s and knew they didn't want it to become dependent on the whims of any telecom providers, the chief information officers of the day took it upon themselves to say, "We're going to aggregate our dollars. We're going to aggregate our skill in high-performance networking, and we're going to create a consortium that can enable a national backbone for the things we need to do. We'll connect it up locally and regionally to get the job done."

They didn't just go to AT&T or to MCI and ask for a proposal; they said they want to own the organization and do business with a bunch of different providers and aggregate the need to procure those services as well as procure expertise over time. I think James and I, over time, saw a lot of similarities. We saw this as an intervention to not let digital education get away from us.

Dave: Why now, with online education? Are we at the right place at the right time for this?

Brad: We're about 18 months behind where I want to be.

James: I'm not sure that the focus is on online education. I think the focus is increasingly on the relationship between teaching and learning. Outcomes are mediated by these technology tools and networks. Even if everything you do is done on campus, it is still the case, and increasingly so, that the whole interaction is mediated by networks and applications. The potential to aggregate our demand and exert some control over what would otherwise become a hostage situation, that is, we would be hostages to the application owners, was part of what drew us to Unizin. That did look very similar to Internet2.

It is also similar in the sense that I don't know how strategic Internet2 membership was or how strategic this consortium is. I am pretty convinced it's essential. A research university that does not have access to high-speed networks via Internet2 is out of the game. It's not that it really gives any real advantage relative to others who are in the game, it's just the price of admission. That is the way I feel about a lot of the stuff that Unizin is trying to deal with. It is the price of admission for teaching and learning in the digital age.

Lois: I will say too I think that the timing is now for those in the lead, as Brad was saying, because of this increased scrutiny on outcomes, on serving new audiences, on understanding the effectiveness of what we're doing. We cannot wait another five years to really understand our businesses in a new and more complete way.

Brad: I would also add to this conversation that the macro sense for our institutions is that education's moving from a public good to a private good. As families and students are paying a greater share of their cost of education, they are more sensitive, price sensitive, et cetera. You see shopping behavior, you see retention and recruiting behavior where the top students or mid-tier students are being chased by the top institutions. I think just hanging out the Indiana University flag for decades was good enough to draw who and what we were looking for. That was true for a lot of leading public institutions, certain private institutions are maybe still there.

I think it's become much more complicated with state funding ramping down and with tuition hikes; we still have escalations of cost, so I think we are having to become much more data driven in response to changes in our external environment.

Lois: At Oregon State, the largest growing demographic is nontraditional learners. We understand that traditional forms of education may not be the best fit, but as we try to design new degree programs, new pacing of programs, new delivery methodologies, new credentialing options, and so on, we're really developing new products. We need data to help guide us on that path to understand what's effective and what will sell.

Dave: Along that line, one of the things I look for from any kind of consortial relationship, especially like the one we are talking about with Unizin, is the support and alliance that helps us keep our eye on the prize. In higher education, we spend a lot of time developing solutions. If we are a hammer, the entire world looks like a nail. We need to spend some time at least understanding who our audiences are and what they want. As an individual institution, under whatever variety of pressures it might have, from administrators, from presidents, from boards of trustees, it is too easy to jump to the solution and not really know what the problem is or might be.

I think it is much harder to resist that kind of solution-based pressure without colleagues and peers you can lean on quickly and easily to help maintain focus. I do not know whether that *only* comes from consortial work, but I think it definitely *does* come from consortial work.

Brad: I think we're still learning what consortial means, but the thing I would also say, when we use the word *consortial*, is we mean loose and tight affiliations. Internet2 is a very loose affiliation: You connect us with a network card, and then whatever each institution does or does not do or pay any attention to, that is really just all your business.

I think, with what we are proposing for the Unizin data platform, we are looking to go fairly far with interdependence. Firms
that really come together and do things in ways that create value
often become fairly interdependent with each other. Microsoft and
Intel have one of the longest standing relationships, two completely
separate, independent entities. They became very interdependent,
not exclusively so, but the vast majority of the products they each
drove for a couple of decades was interdependent.

James: I think that is really important, and I think that is the difference
between a consortium that is just a buyer's club, for example, and
what we've been trying to create. In Unizin, we are intentionally
increasing interdependence, believing that in interdependence
comes strength and presumably advantage downstream, whether it's
because we don't have to buy our content or data back because we
control it, or whether it's because we now have the world's largest learning laboratory, and we can run studies about how effective
teaching and learning are in a variety of situations that we could not
do otherwise.

Somewhere there is maybe a clever twist on all of this, right?
Competitive advantage coming out of intentional interdependence—that is what we are trying to pursue here, and it is the oppo-
site of the way most institution administrators think.

Brad: That is exactly right. That is very much what we're trying to do; that
is an element of interdependence, it requires some new thinking.
Traditionally institution administrators do not think that way.

Dave: We have touched on a couple of factors, interrelationships, and better understanding of the business world as it relates to what we do or
could do and the cycles over time that we go through. What other
factors influence success or failure in something like this? If you were
to put a laundry list together, what factors have an impact on midterm success and long-term success.

Brad: We need the faculty to see and value what the consortium can do for
them. Faculty do not really care what infrastructure or campus costs
are. If we save some money by buying through a consortium, okay,
great. If we do not, okay, great. I think if we can get Unizin to a point
of sophistication, then the faculty can touch it and engage with it
and do data analysis with it, whether it is just in their own class or
among multiple classes. There is value in institutional research for
provosts and other university leaders. If we can gain some advantage on reducing the cost of attendance, how we acquire materials, whether open educational resources or lower publisher prices or

faculty-authored material that is advantageous to our constituents. Frankly in the end, I don't think us crowing about the economics, in the abstract, will win.

I think the faculty will have to see and understand the gain in economics and value that for us to declare this a long-term win. I focus on the faculty and the whole instructional staff. Literally, Unizin is the intel inside because we want the Oregon State or Ohio State or Nebraska brand out front. Much of what learners experience digitally is mediated by faculty choice. That's what we have to influence.

Dave: James, if you were just to run down a similar line, you mentioned interrelationships as a foundation for the largest learning laboratory concept, is this learning laboratory concept built by or with faculty? Is that how we get to the major new ideas? Do we drive that through the faculty?

James: I think that it is driven by our institutions' identities as research institutions. I agree with Brad that long-term success requires faculty adoption. As we keep pushing for the world's largest learning laboratory, we enable faculty to do research they could not do otherwise.

We are playing a short-term and a long-term game here. Being able to just enable research in the short term, for early adopting faculty, is not really enough. We're going to be asked questions about educational effectiveness that cannot be answered in the context of a single institution. I can't tell you how Group X does in science, technology, engineering, and mathematics courses and have it mean anything if I can't do comparisons.

Going back to lessons learned about how to set up a consortium, at least for midterm success, it is about making the stakes high enough that institutions have to care about their investment. I think if we were starting Unizin again, it would be more than a million-dollar commitment across three years. That was a good number, but even so, it's a number that an institution can risk ignoring.

When I look at other consortiums that we have joined or participated in, they often tend to be much lower in commitment, and they immediately fade from visibility to the institution.

Dave: Because basically, you can forget about it, it's not a risk.

James: If the initial commitment is not strong enough, it gets pushed down the priority list. If it is really a strategic move, you do not want to push it so far down the line that it does not hold people's attention.

Again, in some ways, it is the same lesson as Sakai. You want to make sure there is enough of a financial investment to keep the attention of the people who are charged with plotting institutional strategy.

Dave: Just to be crass and blunt about it, is it basically the same corporate issue of "money talks"?

James: I think money does talk. It gets follow-through behavior at the institution—a level of attention that helps the vision succeed.

Brad: Vision easily becomes a casualty from lack of attention or as the first difficulty that is encountered, then it's hard to make a go of it. You know with Sakai, we might have done better if we had tried not to open the tent so fast, if we had made it higher stakes by increasing the initial monetary commitment to join the consortium, and with a smaller number of founding institutions. I do understand James's comment that if we were starting Unizin again, it would be more than a million-dollar commitment across three years, but we thought we were both being pretty damn bold when we made up that number of a million dollars.

James: We did think the price of admission to Unizin was bold and it was, comparatively speaking. But the number keeps going north.

Lois: When we created the Sakai Foundation, and when Brad and others launched the Kuali open source consortium, we operated on a meritocracy principle. The universities that contributed the most resources made the rules. Michigan and Indiana were very large contributors and carried a lot of sway. With Unizin we made everybody an equal contributor, an equal stakeholder in the business. I think there's something a little more contemporary about that model that allows each of us to be an equal stakeholder in the business.

Brad: I think that is right. When you sit down around the Unizin table, you know everybody has bought the same price. Some folks may have invested a little more energy in maturing a product or understanding it, but I am also pretty enamored with how a good bit of that is spread across the consortium. It is great to see some folks working on this tool or that tool, a little earlier, this practice or that practice a little bit better.

Dave: This idea is about the value proposition—I think one of the things you just said, Brad, comes from the fact that we have a common value proposition that we're working on. It's learner success, it's personalized learning at scale, those kinds of things that we can at least characterize similarly together around the table.

One of the issues this consortium faces is multiple lenses. How does my provost view success? What do faculty members see as important to learner success? Do these differing visions have to be reconciled for success, and do we have to bring everybody together in some fashion to generate success? I'm pretty sure, as you have said, the average faculty member is not concerned about what we're doing, and the provost is concerned for different reasons.

Brad: I think there's going to be a heterogeneous view of why someone likes or values Unizin, and I think that's good. That will strengthen us, but it does have to be diverse since not everyone will see the same value proposition in Unizin. I think we have to go deeper into faculty's seeing and perceiving and touching and thinking that something is good, rather than just saying we have a license for a learning platform for campus, to sustain the investment of the money that an institution has invested in Unizin over time.

The counter to that, of course, would be that the faculty do not know what Unizin can offer and they don't care. There is a great data set for those who care; a lot of them do not. Maybe the dashboard could get a little bit better, but over time, those of us who would be charged with building data warehouses and buying analytical tools and cutting these deals to negotiate for the best prices for e-readers, when we look at the alternatives, and we add up the numbers, we turn around and look and say, "Yeah, Unizin is a really good value." Maybe that is enough, but I would sure like for the faculty to know about and understand the things that they value.

James: I agree with all that. I think that there is some advantage to having some heterogeneity of lenses that institutions and their representatives bring. I think there are limits. I think that at one point, relatively early, Unizin flirted with becoming really just a buying club. I think we talked through that, and we did not wind up going down that path. There is still something about trying to aggregate our demand and take some control over our destiny, which I think everybody endorses.

Beyond that, I think it is different by institution. Some institutions are very focused on tools, for example, "Well, I need a dashboard, I need a set of tools, I need a set of metrics that I can turn around and say, 'Look, what happens to my retention, because we now have access to these tools.'" Other places are in Unizin for different reasons. I do not know how to say it other than to recognize that there is a range in which heterogeneity is good, and then there is a range where the risk is in it becoming so heterogeneous that you lose alignment. Concretely, we know we are in danger of losing it the minute any institution starts saying, "This is my do-or-die issue." That is why we spend a lot of time focusing on directional plays over specific tools.

Dave: How do we balance the fact that we have this vision that can be relatively abstract, with the demands for very tangible tools that do something for me today?

Brad: For me I would say that we have got to deliver those tools that are really opportunistic. There is pressure to deliver tools. My provost has said, "I need faculty adopting some of these things, using it." They don't have to praise it necessarily, but they have got to use it. I am all for tools that are directionally consistent, so dashboards are great. Dashboards serve as the eye candy that some institutions and their faculties need. Information technology works really well here. We are about increasingly being data driven in how we approach teaching and learning.

Dave: What does success look like for Unizin five years out?

James: For me, I think it will be the existence of a Unizin data platform one year out, and its expansion over five years, that reflects the principles we have discussed. The creation of the world's largest learning laboratory is incredibly important. We have to drive hard at it, enrich it, and make it accessible to our faculty, because it will be a very unique, rare, valuable, and strategic asset. I think it is the most important thing to pursue and will be an attractor and differentiator over time.

I really hope that Unizin will be able to demonstrate that by sewing multiple parts together at a higher consortial level, in being very intentional about it, we can create a learning environment in which students and faculty interact effectively. I hope it becomes a strategy that has high satisfaction, high level of use, and that it works across any domain that we want for teaching, whether it's massive open online courses or residential or blended or somewhere in between. I think we will be at a very different place from many of our colleagues who decide to go it alone.

It seems to me, if we fast-forward five years, that our success should illustrate why choosing to become interdependent creates strong value. It should serve as a reference point that demonstrates the value of the consortium path. People don't know what the efficacies of those two different paths are yet.

Lois: I agree, and I think that not being complacent is a part of this as well. We're in our first wave of value-added tools for our faculty and students with the readers and publishers and dashboards and so on. What I would like to see in five years is that we are really quite adept at bringing in new products, new features, new methods of teaching in a way that meets our university's needs. Our portfolio of tools in Unizin will continue to evolve more quickly and more adeptly than it has ever done before.

James: I think if I had to pick a single thing that will demonstrate success, it is the data platform—I think of it as a data observatory. I think what Unizin is building is highly differentiated and incredibly hard to replicate. It is a rich, shared data warehouse that allows us to basically perform all kinds of studies, answer all kinds of questions and increasingly drives the tools that come out of it. It's difficult for me to imagine a more valuable asset than a rich data set of about a million students across a diverse set of institutions. Imagine what you could do with that. One of the linchpin examples of this kind of asset is the Panel Study of Income Dynamics at the Institute for Social Research (2018). This is a 30-year study that continues to generate value. I don't see anybody else doing this. I see private companies trying to lock data up. They will give you a black box and spit out some results if you are willing to pay enough, but the idea of doing this kind of study as university-based consortium where scientists do the analysis in an open, transparent, and scaled way to answer questions in data-driven ways is the holy grail we are chasing.

Brad: I think that is really important, and I do not know that we have really put the message out, that Unizin is melding our two missions— our education mission and our research mission. That is probably an important thing for us to learn to communicate better, after we have a little evidence to show that it is true. Again, the management strategy folks write about things that really enable differentiation and value in companies. Sometimes they write about what are called VRIN capabilities: valuable, rare, inimitable, and nonsubstitutable. If you do not have them, you cannot define or enable differentiation and value. I see the Unizin data platform as a VRIN resource for the consortium members. That's what it takes for a great consortium and what we are focused on for Unizin.

References

Institute for Social Research. (2018). *Panel study for income dynamics*. Retrieved from
  https://psidonline.isr.umich.edu
Senge, P. (2006). *The fifth discipline: The art and practice of the learning organization*.
  New York, NY: Doubleday.

5

EFFECTIVELY LEADING INNOVATION

Thomas Cavanagh and Luke Dowden

Creating a culture of innovation takes effective leadership. This chapter addresses the experiences of building, nurturing, and sustaining teams that can produce award-winning innovations. In particular, this chapter describes strategies and practices that help to ensure clear communication, professional development, coordination, and creativity among team members, as well as the structures and organizational cultures required for effectively leading innovation. Contextual factors include organizational structures, business operations, strategic investments, human resources, start-up, and sustaining financing. Cultural factors address the academic governance, the environment and appetite for innovation, and the building blocks that support change management and sustain successes. These various factors can be categorized into the following set of organizing principles that help to establish a culture of innovation in e-learning leadership:

- Keeping your edge: The art of being stretched
- Location, location, location: The organizational chart matters
- The people in the machine: The importance of human resources
- Risk and reward: Accelerating change and mitigating issues
- Are we there yet? Developing clear metrics for success
- Knowing when to hold 'em and when to fold 'em: Reinvestment, renewal, and pivots

Background

The role of the institutional online leader has been increasing in profile and influence in recent years. As documented by Fredricksen (2017), a growing number of institutions have established key senior administrative positions to strategically manage their digital learning operations. Salisbury (2017) identifies three key roles on successful higher education innovation teams: the leader, the champion, and the founder. Although no single set of titles has yet been established to represent these institutional roles, the expectations and skill sets seem to all coalesce around the same types of traditional leadership attributes.

Understanding the process of innovation is an important prerequisite, such as Matchley's (2017) six steps for innovation. Perhaps even more important, Matchley identifies five common traits for innovators: curiosity and creativity, integrative thinking, collaboration, connectors, and perseverance and grit. One key theme that emerges for successful oversight of postsecondary online learning is the ability to manage innovation. A fundamental prerequisite is the ability to see the broader context of innovation and develop a framework for managing it in an individual institution, such as proposed by Dugdale and Strawn (2017). They suggest "viewing the campus as an Innovation Landscape" (para. 2) and creating a culture that supports innovation across various domains.

Perhaps this last point—creating a culture that fosters and supports innovation—is the most crucial of any skill required of an online learning leader. With the speed of technological change accelerating at a breakneck pace, it can sometimes be difficult to consider the long-range innovations required for future growth while managing the day-to-day requirements of general operations (Cavanagh & Thompson, 2017). Setser and Morris (2015) describe the critical need for creating a culture of innovation in higher education, especially in light of exploding technological advancement and change happening faster than the ability to predict and strategize.

So what can online learning leaders do to ensure they keep up with the requirements of rapidly changing innovation? This chapter proposes a series of practical strategies that can be employed to foster and support innovation in a higher education context. They are not intended to be sequential, nor will all be entirely applicable for all contexts. Yet these have proven to be effective methods for us and should have broader utility for most online learning leaders.

Keeping Your Edge: The Art of Being Stretched

In the world of fitness and athletic training, participants must continually push their abilities and endurance past the point of comfort in order to improve. It is only by stretching, by pushing beyond previously established levels of achievement that athletes can reach new levels. The same is true in the world of digital learning. Online learning leaders need to continually be reaching beyond their grasp, stretching to accomplish greater impact.

This may mean establishing standard and stretch goals for key metrics, such as students served, faculty trained, courses delivered, money saved, student success, or any other goals that are key for a unit's relevance to the institutional mission. Being stretched is important for the leader and the team being led. The leader should set an example through transparently sharing personal goals such as professional development, training, and other strategies for expanding knowledge and skills. Likewise, the leader should also make departmental goals clear and transparent and allow individual teams members to suggest ways they can help achieve such goals.

Although it is important to set ambitious goals, the leader must walk a fine line between establishing targets that are too easily met (thereby reducing job satisfaction because of a lack of challenge and creating no sense of accomplishment) and reaching for targets that are clearly unrealistic (thus discouraging staff and negatively affecting morale). Stretch goals should be difficult but achievable. The leader should also help to identify paths that can be taken to accomplish challenging goals. The leader should also serve as the unit's advocate and ensure that the resources are available to meet the challenge. Arbitrarily setting a difficult goal without providing the means for accomplishing it would result in worse outcomes and, if repeated, would spiral with loss of staff and a departmental culture of no confidence.

Establishing a challenging objective is an ideal opportunity to encourage staff to be creative. It can be difficult to accomplish new goals through existing means. Simply working harder isn't typically effective in the long term. Innovation is the means by which teams can consider new ways to accomplish new goals. That's why the online learning leader must create a culture where it is safe to fail. As Matchley (2017) says, "innovation is also a way of thinking and collaboration and, yes, failure" (para. 14). Innovation is not a linear process; it requires starts and stops, backtracks and dead-ends. But teams must feel they have the space to explore new processes and technologies, for that is where longer term success may lie. Thus, if stretch goals are not met, but teams are creating new ideas for solving new problems in new ways, the leader must publicly recognize the value of these efforts.

Location, Location, Location: The Organizational Chart Matters

An old axiom in the world of real estate states that the three most important features of a property are location, location, and location. An argument can be made that the same holds true for an online learning leader who wants to encourage and leverage institutional innovation. Where a digital learning leader resides on the organizational chart informs the broader campus community about the importance of the role to the institution. This position can help convey a sense of urgency and strategic importance when building coalitions for initiatives and communicates that the institution's senior leadership is behind the efforts.

According to Fredricksen (2017), 52% of chief online learning officers report directly to the provost, and 5% report directly to the president. Salisbury (2017) refers to these roles as champions, describing them as follows:

> Champions should report directly to a president or provost and are often bestowed with glitzy titles like Chief Innovation Officer or Vice Provost for Innovation & Education. They are seasoned—and senior—participants in university life and culture. As pros in navigating institutional process and politics, they align the resources and partners necessary for new initiatives to take root and grow. A champion's primary charge is building buy-in and momentum for the innovation agenda. (para. 11)

Such a reporting structure sends a message about the value placed on online learning. This can be useful for a digital learning leader who is experimenting with new technologies and processes. Sometimes, the biggest hurdle in implementing an innovation is cultural—for example, being told that's not how it has always been done. As Salisbury (2017) states, champions often "describe their job as 90 percent convincing people there is reason and urgency for the institution to innovate, and 10 percent actually building things" (para. 12). Although true leadership comes from the individual and the credibility earned through experience and trust, the positional authority that accompanies a reporting structure can be a useful tool in accomplishing goals.

If an online learning leader does not report to a provost or president, the leader can still innovate and accomplish necessary goals. Fredricksen (2017) also states that 23% of online learning leaders report to another senior academic leader, whereas 7% report to a nonacademic vice president, 5% to a chief information officer, and 3% to a dean of a school. Such organizational placement can still wield considerable influence and tap necessary resources. At the end of the day, while valuable, positional authority is of less long-term value than individual reputation. It is always possible to lead from where you are.

The People in the Machine: The Importance of Human Resources

Innovation is a uniquely human enterprise. Human resources are essential to convene, connect, and do the work of an intermediary inside the organization.

The online learning leader needs competent staff as the leader must be able to rely on team members who understand the institution's culture and context. *Success in innovation*, defined as sustaining the innovation or disinvesting from it, relies on strong relationships with a wide range of stakeholders. The business of innovating is about people connecting to each other around a common purpose. Keeping people connected across the organization and in spite of their differences is the hallmark of a successful leader. This topic delves into some additional detail around selecting staff, developing coalitions of the willing and doing, cultivating executive advocates, and operating through transparency.

Intensive Staff Selection
An online learning leader's overall success will depend on how well the leader can assemble a talented cast. Selecting staff is the most important job of the chief online learning officer. To acquire talent, one must make the case to the decision makers about why the positions are needed and show the vision for maximizing human resources. The goal of the following hiring process is to identify people the online learning leader wants to work with and who knows they want to work in the online learning unit in the organization. It is an intense experience for the candidate, the staff, and the hiring manager. A process that has worked quite well for us includes the following phases:

Phase 1: Application solicitation. Be clear about the position that is open and provide examples of a typical workday. Spend the time to clearly and accurately define the position and the experiences and skills you desire. Ask applicants to submit documents in a specific way. Failure to follow the submission instructions eliminates those who do not follow directions.

Phase 2: Application review. Involving staff in the application review allows them to envision how each candidate might fit as part of the team. The application review is a great opportunity to engage staff in a most important decision-making process and gives staff practice with hiring. The online learning leader challenges staff reviewers to look for information in each application that aligns with the education and work experience described in the position posting. No limits on the number of applicants moving to the next phase are set. An opportunity for all team members to share findings and value the recommendations of others is facilitated by the online learning leader.

Phase 3: The phone interview. As part of the invitation to participate in the phone interview, information is provided on the department's culture and accomplishments. The salary range for the position is given, clearly stipulating that the salary is or is not negotiable. Candidates are invited to opt out if the range does not match their expectations. The phone interview phase of the staff selection process allows the hiring manager to have a unique interaction with a candidate of interest. Moreover, the candidate has an opportunity to evaluate the unit. Phone interview questions should attempt to illuminate each candidate's understanding of the position; uncover their work style, ideal work environment, and environmental stressors; and provide candidates with an opportunity to demonstrate their values and self-awareness. The phone interview allows the online learning leader to expressly focus on words and tone—not gender, not ethnicity, not body language. The point is to have some conversation with candidates before the committee interview.

Phase 4: Scenario response (live demonstration). Based on the phone interviews and another look at the application file, a smaller, select group of applicants is invited to participate in a response to a scenario. This phase allows applicants to prove they have the requisite knowledge and skills in the position's description. The staff in the subunits most closely related to the open position help design the scenario to solve a problem of the day. The problem is complex, but not overwhelming, with clear parameters on how to respond within a given time line. This step is all about problem-solving. How does the candidate approach the challenge? What creative methods does the candidate employ? Is the solution achievable? Does the candidate ask for help? A well-structured scenario will allow the best candidates to show their most complete set of skills.

Phase 5: Face-to-face interview with a committee. Hosting a face-to-face or synchronous interview is as important as the members of the committee. The committee members can be from the organization's industry councils or the institution's strategic online or digital learning council. Online learning leaders form committees they can trust. They listen to the committee's input even when tempted to ignore advice if the online learning leader has developed a strong interest in a particular candidate. The previous phases should have produced three to four high-quality candidates. If the candidates are strong, and if the committee is balanced by careful selection, then committee members will make a recommendation of a high-quality candidate to best fit the identified needs and add value to the team.

After such a rigorous process, the online learning leader rewards a new hire with a defined onboarding road map, which includes stated performance milestones and scheduled 30-day, 60-day, and 90-day performance reviews. For teams with a larger staff, the online learning leader should assign a staff mentor.

Developing Coalitions of the Willing and Doing
Hiring staff is only part of the human resources strategy the digital learning leader needs to implement for success in the business of online learning.

Coalitions of the willing and doing are required. An industry council or an institution-wide digital or online learning council represent the more formal coalitions. These groups are tasked to help the online learning leader expand thought leadership. These councils do the heavy lifting on policy creation and adoption, process development and improvement, and advocacy when the online learning leader confronts opportunities and threats. User groups and communities of interest are other forms of formal coalitions of the willing.

Informal coalitions are equally important. Sometimes referred to as *coalitions of the doing*, these networks emerge from the tireless efforts of a chief online learning officer to spend time with different constituent groups. Informal coalitions should include an engaged network of deans, department heads, faculty, and student services administrators who will defend the innovations and changes to processes and learning experiences. Their role is essential as they manage the hallway conversations, the water cooler rumors, and become a mentor to others in their roles. These coalitions provide internal validity. They also provide a level of accountability to the online learning leader by alerting the leader to systemic concerns or emerging issues the online learning leader may be unaware of or not fully informed about.

Cultivating Executive Advocates

Executive advocates are essential to an online learning leader's success. These individuals help frame messages, determine timing for requests, formulate strategies to advance initiatives, prepare leaders for difficult conversations, alert leaders when they wander off course, coach leaders when they fail, call attention to blind spots, and communicate wins to key stakeholders. Developing competency in cultivating executive advocates is vital for the success of the online learning leader. Innovating inside a higher education institution can be a messy experience because there are many variables the leader cannot control, especially actions of others. Executive advocates navigate the organization's complexity with online learning leaders. Depending on the level of the online leader's position in the organization, the importance of and strategies employed to cultivate executive advocates will differ. Yet there are some basic approaches to consider.

The chief online learning officer's direct supervisor is the first and most important executive advocate. If any other advocate is more informed than one's direct supervisor, then sufficient time is not being spent to inform the supervisor. Leaders should not assume that their supervisor understands or supports online learning. Conversely, the supervisor will help the online learning leader understand how the chain of command works to make the approval process more efficient and can act as a buffer to shield the online enterprise from internal issues.

Meeting regularly with one's supervisor and other executive advocates should be a routine habit. Scheduling brief check-ins with executive advocates ensures ongoing dialogue of key issues and strategies to overcome them. The online learning leader is advised to keep the list of topics to a minimum and to focus on the most pressing items to produce actionable results. The most important next step after each engagement with an executive advocate is to send a thank-you note, review agreed-on actions, and set the next meeting. Success as a leader in innovating online will depend on a diverse set of executive advocates in key positions across the college or university.

Operating Through Transparency

Successful chief online learning officers operate well through transparency. Consistency is the first rule of thumb. Having a communication and convening strategy with transparency as a core value is the second rule of thumb. The following are other applicable rules of engagement to more effectively operate through transparency.

Be visible and accessible. The online learning leader cannot be transparent if they are not present. Visibility on campus is directly linked to the leader's success with advocating for the online and digital learning enterprise. Taking an active part in opportunities outside the digital learning department is important to increase the leader's own awareness of the institution's changing culture and context. Engagement on issues of institutional importance that may not be directly related to online or digital learning helps the leader gain trust from the community and prevents an isolationist view of the leader. This strategy is especially important if the leader manages a self-support unit that depends on departments to provide courses and programs. Because an institution's culture and contexts shift, an engaged leader can adjust strategies and the narrative more quickly. Present leaders do not assume that faculty, staff, and administrators know and understand the contributions the leader makes to the larger teaching and learning enterprise.

Convene and connect stakeholders. Operating through transparency means convening and connecting internal stakeholders. It requires developing an ability to have uncomfortable and awkward conversations. For transparency to work, the leader focuses on processes rather than criticizing people. Depending on the topic or group members, the online learning leader needs to be honest about the challenges faced or opportunities recognized. Thoughtful framing of the issues is pivotal to keep the focus on the purpose, such as student success or satisfaction. By asking for help, the online learning leader engages and empowers others in the task of defining the solutions. Transparent online learning leaders communicate equitably by ensuring everyone has the same information. The enemies of transparency are lack of information, misinformation, or uneven distribution of information needed for group members to give their best ideas and solutions.

Risk and Reward: Accelerating Change and Mitigating Issues

Ideally, the university will have a defined culture on change, how it is managed, and how issues are mitigated. An institution can severely stifle consistent gains if change management and parameters for risk are not defined at the highest level by the president or provost. The most innovative institutions garnering the highest online enrollments have identified a blend of innovating at scale while not completely disrupting the successful educational delivery systems that each is sustaining. These institutions were not created to change, yet they have adapted structures and empowered leaders to innovate on the side of production. Most important, the chief online learning leader is integrating new developments by incubating new course designs, technologies, and pedagogies through action research centers with a specific mission to take instructional risks with emerging technologies and pedagogies. These centers are using a combination of frameworks and tools such as design thinking, sprints, failing at scale, and pilots.

Design thinking. Design thinking uses a nonlinear process and tool sets to discover, emphasize, prototype, test, and evaluate changes in services, products, or instruction. According to Brown (2016), creative leadership requires a leader to "unlock the creative potential" in the organization to "set the conditions for an organization to generate, embrace, and execute on new ideas" (para. 5). Successful online learning leaders are introducing and actively using design thinking techniques to address their wicked problems.

Sprints. Some market force, leadership change, or new product will require swift action and clear results. When the online learning leader needs to adapt quickly, sprinting may be the most appropriate change mechanism. According to Schwaber and Sutherland (2016), "Each sprint may be considered a project with no more than a one-month horizon. Each sprint has a definition of what is to be built, a design and flexible plan that will guide building it, the work, and the resultant product." (p. 8). Course design sprints, which sometimes occur as a set of sprints, are popular when launching new programs.

Failing at scale. One emerging model of changing quickly to improve outcomes or to gain market share is the concept of fail at scale. Online learning leaders have aggressive time lines to move an innovation from design to rapid deployment to affect the greatest number of learners in the shortest, most efficient amount of time. Arizona State University's EdPlus celebrates this mission of "education at scale and speed for everyone, everywhere"

(EdPlus at Arizona State University, n.d.) Again, the online learning leader will consider this strategy when the benefits of an innovation outweigh the risks and the pains of change.

Pilots. When the online learning leader questions claims of a new product, technology, or instructional strategy, pilots are useful. The online learning leader needs a suitable pilot size to evaluate potential impact and to provide opportunities for the community to support the venture. If the leaders opt for a pilot-to-tell strategy, a critical, initial decision must determine how many pilots will be pursued before an innovation is abandoned or scaled. Otherwise, pilots become the end goal rather than advancing the learning experience for students.

Accelerating change and mitigating issues require proven strategies that empower the online learning leader to incentivize risk. The most innovative institutions of higher education have created these frameworks or used the following strategies: nurtured, creative judgement-free zones; embedded risk takers in active communities of inquiry; identified clear exit strategies; and designed infrastructures to rapidly scale innovation. Finally, offering options for different pathways that projects may follow to evolve is an important strategy for online learning leaders when recommending projects to the institution's executive leadership team.

Balancing Strategic and Operational Demands

As an online learning enterprise reaches scale, imbalances between strategy and operations can emerge. The imbalance may occur from the start or grow steadily or unevenly over time. Any sustained imbalance can result in unwanted consequences such as the online program leaders' becoming risk averse, course and program designs stagnating, pedagogies and technological solutions losing relevance, and overall competitiveness and market share of the institution's online learning program waning. The chief online learning leader must be well equipped and supported in balancing the strategic and operational needs of leading innovation.

Over time, strategic and operational priorities will compete more aggressively for the leader's time and energy. Mike Abbiatti, the Western Interstate Commission for Higher Education's vice president for educational technologies and executive director of the Western Interstate Commission for Higher Education's Cooperative for Educational Technologies, uses a simple and effective formula for evaluating initiatives, which is his form of selecting strategic initiatives and conducting a resource capacity needs assessment (M. Abbiatti, personal communication, 2016). Before an investment or commitment is made, he asks his staff to answer these four questions when the group is evaluating any project or tool: Do our members need it? Can we staff it? Can we afford it? What is our exit strategy? There is a delicate balance among sustaining innovation, which is no longer an innovation; disengaging from a project; and engaging in projects on the horizon without pushing all your chips into one direction.

The larger and more sustained an online learning enterprise becomes, the more operational tasks may dominate the online learning leader's time, energy, and workload. Kaplan and Norton (2008) warn that failure to balance strategy and operations will result in a firsthand experience with Gresham's law: "Discussions about bad operations inevitably drive out discussions about good strategy implementation" (p. 64). Tools to periodically evaluate the balance are essential for short-term and long-term success. Although neither can be neglected, creating a system for understanding when to prioritize strategy and when to prioritize operations is critical. Using some form of a closed-loop management system allows the online learning leader to continue pursuing strategic risks and innovations while sustaining successful operations (Kaplan & Norton, 2008).

To further balance the strategic and operational demands of leading an online learning enterprise, the chief online learning leader must develop and rely on a network of peers. For this network, the leader should identify seasoned higher education administrators and faculty members willing to serve as formal and informal mentors. Developing professional relationships with mentors provides a healthy outlet for the leader to seek honest evaluations of ideas or strategies, to receive guidance on dealing with difficult situations, and to gain advice when major decisions are imminent. Innovating inside the online learning enterprise without engaging outside experts can place the leader in a distorted reality bubble. Mentors can help online learning leaders get out of their own way by inviting them outside their bubble.

Time to equip others for success is another competitor of the online learning leader's time. Empowering team members to take ownership and to exercise initiative must remain a top priority. No management system can reach full operational efficiency without capacity building in the leader's team. Successful online learning leaders create a work environment built on investing in staff members' professional development, showcasing their talents, and pushing each beyond their individual comfort zones. Making time to listen to and support staff on the front lines will inform the leader of severe process friction for faculty, students, and staff. Moreover, listening time can reveal misalignments with the strategy and how the strategy may have been misinterpreted.

Frontline professional staff solve problems on a daily basis, manage student complaints, and survive deficiencies in processes, systems, and other personnel. Yet the support staff may not always be able to spot a systemic program or determine the best solution or feel empowered to manage up. The online learning leader should provide tools or mechanisms that empower the support. Five to Ten Tag Me In is an empowering guideline for frontline support staff to alert supervisors to the potential of a systemic issue after observing and documenting the same issue 5 to 10 times. Depending on the issue, procedures may need to be adjusted to lower the number of incidents before they are reported. The key is establishing operational parameters that encourage frontline staff to manage up. Online learning leaders need to establish a culture where mistakes are valued as learning moments.

Are We There Yet? Developing Clear Metrics for Success

How do the chief online officers know when they are successful? What gets measured? Who measures it? Why does it matter? The innovative chief online leader considers these questions often. Clear performance metrics and target results must exist for an online learning enterprise to succeed. These metrics might include percentage of market share, enrollment in online programs, enrollment in noncredit learning experiences, percentage improvements in retention of certain programs, completion targets, and grants awarded. Knowing when some measure of success has been reached is important. As Kotter (1996) points out, "Whenever you let up before the job is done, critical momentum can be lost and regression may follow" (p. 133).

A plan to periodically revisit success metrics and refine them must exist from the beginning. For example, if an expectation is for the online learning operation to be a self-funded unit, a target date for this achievement and stair-stepped milestones are needed. Spending time with stakeholders and clarifying metrics can mitigate disillusionment, which occurs when disparate expectations are not merged or aligned. Moreover, the online learning leader needs the right tools to measure results of the strategic and operational plans. A strategy map, balanced scorecard, and catalog of strategic expenditures are some tools to measure the success of the strategic plan. Dashboards, budgets, pro formas by program, and profit and loss statements are tools to measure results of the operating plan (Kaplan & Norton, 2008).

To achieve established metrics, an institution of higher education must define its tolerance for risk and loss. Tension exists in the space between risk and success. Online learning leaders want to understand the price of failure, specifically the consequences for the next innovation attempted. Conversely, faculty and academic program directors want to know the investment the institution will make in its online program before development and launch. More important, these groups collectively want their runway for success defined in terms of how many months or years are planned to hit their targets, whether enrollment or excess revenue over expenses or some other metric. The institution will not be able to respond without evaluating its own tolerance for risk and loss. Engaging in a conversation on this topic early, often, and continuously with the institution's executive leadership will enable the chief online learning officer to advance initiatives with the most current expectations and adapt metrics for success as needed.

Knowing When to Hold 'Em and When to Fold 'Em: Reinvestment, Renewal, and Pivots

In any innovation portfolio, it is necessary to periodically evaluate the mix of initiatives and determine the status of each one. Has a particular project shown sufficient promise to warrant additional new investment to bring it to scale? Does a project require an extended time line to allow for further evaluation? Should a project be put on a watch list for possible sunsetting? Does the project require a shift in approach or a change in project leadership? Should a project be terminated? These are all questions that must be asked, and the innovative online learning leader should articulate a process for continual program evaluation. After all, no one exists in a world of unlimited resources, and hard, data-driven decisions must be made about where to invest time, funding, and staff expertise.

The ultimate goal of many projects is to scale them for maximum impact. Can what began as a pilot or boutique project be used for wider student success or reduced cost or improved graduation rates or any other key institutional objective? Although there may be nothing wrong with a one-off boutique innovation project, keeping it at the expense of something else that may have greater institutional impact may not be possible. Leaders must be capable of making tough decisions for the greater good of the institution.

The University of Maryland University College has developed an effective process for evaluating project viability and making decisions about continuation or termination through a framework of leading indicators (Ford & Goodall, 2016). These indicators include such topics as interest, value proposition, vendor relationship, trailblazers, and communication. Combined with data from coincident indicators and lagging indicators, the college can make data-informed decisions about project viability.

Sometimes a project may end up heading in an unforeseen direction. When this occurs, the project team should pause and assess why. In some cases, a course correction may be necessary to get back on track. However, in other cases, such a development may be indicative that the project is evolving. It is said that scientists at 3M (2018) accidentally discovered Post-it Notes. In reality, they were trying to develop a very strong adhesive but wound up with a very weak one. It took years, but eventually 3M was able to pivot the project to capitalize on the accident and developed Post-it Notes (3M, 2018). Likewise, the digital learning leader should be open minded enough to see when a failure in one area could be a success in another. Is an innovation being used in an unanticipated way? Can the project be redirected to address the newly identified need? Sometimes the broader community will communicate what it needs, even if it isn't explicitly articulated. The innovative leader needs to be able to hear that message and know when to pivot a project to meet a new need.

It is never easy to terminate an initiative. Such a decision could result from any number of possible reasons. It could be because of technology changes that render the current approach obsolete. The project might be successful on a small scale but is not able to support the infrastructure or costs associated with wider adoption. Perhaps even after revising the approach or changing the team, the results are still not as hoped for, and the project has become a drain on resources. Perhaps the pilot simply didn't work. As stated before, the only way innovation can be achieved is by creating a safe space for failure.

Conclusion

Driving innovation is a complex task for any digital learning leader. However, simply managing existing day-to-day operations, although important, is insufficient to stay relevant in the current climate of rapid technological change and evolving business models. Fostering and supporting innovation depends on core components in any effective online learning leader's skill set. The strategies presented in this chapter are not intended to be a step-by-step process toward that end. Rather, as a whole they point toward a continual cycle of evaluation and adjustment, supporting a process that strives for steady improvement. Innovation inherently involves setbacks. The determined digital learning leader will not let setbacks derail progress toward a vision. Recognition that expanded goals and new capabilities will usually not be realized through existing methods is essential. Pushing boundaries, challenging assumptions, building new technologies, and developing creative processes will be necessary. The leader of innovation will establish the team, culture, structure, and resources required to bring about the digital education of tomorrow.

References

3M. (2018). *History timeline: Post-it Notes*. Retrieved from https://www.post-it .com/3M/en_US/post-it/contact-us/about-us/

Brown, T. (2016, May 16). Unlock your organization's creative potential [Web log post]. Retrieved from https://designthinking.ideo.com/?p=1474

Cavanagh, T., & Thompson, K. (2017). Keeping FIRRST things first: The delicate dance of leading online innovation at your institution. In A. A. Piña, V. L. Lowell, & B. R. Harris (Eds.), *Leading and managing e-Learning: What the e-Learning leader needs to know* (pp. 1–12). New York, NY: Springer.

Dugdale, S., & Strawn, B. (2017, February 13). Crafting an innovation landscape. *EDUCAUSE Review.* Retrieved from https://er.educause.edu/articles/2017/2/crafting-an-innovation-landscape

EdPlus at Arizona State University. (n.d.). *The power of EdPlus.* Retrieved November 03, 2017, from https://edplus.asu.edu/

Ford, C., & Goodall, S. (2016, May). *Leading indicators for successful innovations.* Paper presented at the meeting of the Instructional Management System Global Learning Impact Leadership Institute, San Antonio, TX.

Fredricksen, E. E. (2017). A national study of online learning leaders in US higher education. *Online Learning, 21*(2). Retrieved from http://dx.doi.org/10.24059/olj.v21i2.1164

Kaplan, R. S., & Norton, D.P. (2008, January). Mastering the management system. *Harvard Business Review.* Retrieved from https://hbr.org/2008/01/mastering-the-management-system#comment-section

Kotter, J. P. (1996). *Leading change.* Boston, MA: Harvard Business School Press.

Matchley, R. (2017). Six steps to innovation. *EDUCAUSE Review 52*(4), 8–9.

Salisbury, A. D. (2017, October 11). Inside the incubators: The anatomy of a university innovation team. *EdSurge.* Retrieved from https://www.edsurge.com/news/2017-10-11-inside-the-incubators-the-anatomy-of-a-university-innovation-team

Schwaber, K., & Sutherland, J. (2016). *The scrum guide.* Retrieved from http://www.scrumguides.org/index.html

Setser, B., & Morris, H. (2015). Building a culture of innovation in higher education: Design & practice for leaders. *EDUCAUSE.* Retrieved from https://library.educause.edu/~/media/files/library/2015/4/ngt1502-pdf.pdf

6

MAKING INNOVATION STICK

Phil Regier and Kathryn Scheckel

One of the challenges of sustaining a culture of innovation is the integration of innovations into the day-to-day practices of an organization. In this chapter, we discuss not only the importance of being open to new ideas but also how to make those ideas stick in an institution of higher education. Using the groundbreaking collaboration between Arizona State University (ASU) and Starbucks as an archetype, we provide practical strategies for how to create sustainable innovations that become embedded in an institutional framework and can lead to future creative endeavors.

The culture and vision of a company based not on the products it produces but on the connections it fosters exemplifies Starbucks's commitment to inspire and nurture the human spirit. These values are visible at each Starbucks's storefront, counter, and cup. They permeate each interaction across each of the more than 29,000 Starbucks stores globally, where more than 277,000 people proudly wear the green apron.

Howard Schultz, former chief executive officer and current chairman emeritus of Starbucks, served as the chief architect of Starbucks's mission for more than three decades. A primary example of Starbucks's investment in the human spirit is providing health care benefits and company stock for part-time and full-time workers. This same commitment to the health, well-being, and the future of its employees led Starbucks to launch the Starbucks College Achievement Plan (SCAP) in partnership with ASU. SCAP is an innovative education benefit that allows eligible Starbucks employees (referred to as *partners*) to attend ASU at no tuition to obtain a college degree.

Conceptualized through a close partnership between Schultz and ASU President Michael Crow, and implemented by teams at both enterprises,

SCAP went from an idea in a conversation to a full program within nine months. According to Crow,

> "The [Starbucks] College Achievement Plan has been a powerful demonstration of what is possible when an enlightened and innovative corporation joins forces with a forward-thinking research university. This program is a clear expression of Starbucks' commitment to its employees and ASU's continuing mission to provide access to higher education to all qualified students." ("Starbucks and ASU Offer Four Years of College with Full Tuition Coverage," 2015, para. 5)

At Starbucks and ASU, teams with experience, vision, and drive set out to design and implement this new higher education benefit. In the case of ASU, the innovative culture and engine of team members have grown relatively quickly over the past 15 years. In the case of Starbucks, its innovative spirit has been maturing for more than three decades.

Throughout this chapter, we discuss the history of ASU and how its partnership with Starbucks led to the implementation of this revolutionary twenty-first-century education benefit for Starbucks's partners. We discuss what it means to be innovative in higher education and how to make innovation stick in complex, matrixed organizations. We also provide key ideas for leaders in education to foster unique partnerships and build programs to last.

Shared Values Give Rise to Innovation and Change

Innovation is not something that appears overnight. It develops over time, sometimes in a few years and other times over decades. This is evident in studying ASU and Starbucks each as separate institutions and together as a change agent. A true culture of innovation is one that constantly grows, matures, and adapts. When there is institutional support at the highest levels for such a culture, then people affiliated with all the required resources—strategy, finances, human capital, and others—innovate together. Conversely, an individual or group in an institution may have a superior idea, strategy, or finances, but without the right cultural mind-set, new projects can fail or underachieve. The cultural mind-set to experiment and take risks and be rewarded for experimenting is very much shared across Starbucks and ASU.

Over the past 15 years, ASU has grown from 50,000 students to more than 100,000. The number of students ASU graduates annually has tripled, and the academic quality and outcomes of its degree programs have increased. As a comprehensive public research university, ASU measures itself not by whom it excludes but rather by whom it includes and how those individuals succeed. The administration, faculty, and staff believe that all qualified students who seek a college degree should have access to one. Building a culture of inclusivity as well as a culture of partnerships has allowed ASU to continue its growth for on-campus and online students.

From the first Starbucks store at Pike Place Market in Seattle, Washington, which opened in 1971, to now more than 29,000 stores in countries around the world, Starbucks has experienced rapid growth in a relatively short history as a public company ("Number of Starbucks Stores Worldwide From 2003 to 2018," 2018). With his leadership team, Schultz shaped and redefined the role of a public company beginning in the 1980s as he and his team defined an American coffee experience. For Starbucks to be successful in its mission "to inspire and nurture the human spirit—one person, one cup and one neighborhood at a time" (Starbucks Coffee Company, 2018a), it must build emotional connections between its partners and customers, meaning that its partners are truly at the heart of Starbucks's success. In 1987 Starbucks was one of the first major for-profit corporations to offer health care benefits to part-time workers ("Coffee Czar: Executive Chairman, Former CEO, Starbucks," 2017). It was a radical move then and was followed by many other companies over time.

Related History Leading to Shared Passion

Deep personal experiences are often the roots that produce change agents, sparking innovation and making it stick particularly in complex organizations like for-profit companies and institutions of higher education.

In Schultz's (1997) case, he was inspired to tackle a challenge he saw looming in the United States: the rising debt among Americans pursuing a college degree. He saw how this debt and the growing economic inequality between the working class and the elite pushed access to a university-level education further out of reach. From the beginning, Schultz witnessed firsthand how his Starbucks partners made the choice to work instead of attend school.

Schultz grew up in public housing in Brooklyn. His father worked a job that gave him no dignity or meaning. The elder Schultz suffered a serious injury that left him out of work with no health insurance or worker's compensation to hold the family together financially (Schultz, 1997).

A similar focus on the challenges of access to education is constantly on the mind of ASU's Crow, the sixteenth president of the youngest major research institution and largest university governed by a single administration in the United States. Crow is all too familiar with the difficult personal choice to attend college. The first in his family to attend college, his passion for learning grew in his university classroom. The son of an enlisted sailor, Crow grew up all around the United States, moving 21 times before attending college. His mother passed away when Crow was only 9 years old, leaving his father to raise 5 children alone (Crow, 2016).

Crow often speaks of an event in 1968 that changed the focus and trajectory of his life. An aspiring Eagle Scout, Crow and his friend collected a year's supply of food, holiday toys, and gifts for a needy family near his Maryland home. Crow's father helped pack a U-Haul truck to deliver the goodies to the eager recipients, huddled on their dirt floor under a tar-paper roof. Later that day, in the rundown living room of the government housing where he lived, Crow watched in amazement as astronauts of the Apollo 8 spaceflight mission flew around the moon. The intense dichotomy between his morning and his evening left a mark on young Crow. He recalls thinking, "Who were these people living in a shack; who were we; and who were these people up at the moon?" (Crow, 2016, para. 10). This dual notion of unfairness and the sense that anything was possible with education drove Crow to Iowa State University, where he studied political science and environmental science. His childhood experiences fed his desire to innovate and make a university education possible for anyone, anywhere: "College created this incredible environment for me to learn in the widest possible way" (Crow, 2016, para. 20).

Passion for innovation and like-minded values can also be a driving factor in the development of partnerships. In the case of Starbucks and ASU, leaders and team members of both organizations share the vision that everyone deserves the opportunity to obtain a great education and that every employee should feel valued in the workplace. The alignment in vision and perspective between Schultz and Crow laid the foundation for a new way of thinking about corporate social responsibility. A new kind of partnership between a global for-profit company and a public university was born and was destined to enable people to achieve success through higher education because it is the right thing to do.

Creating a Twenty-First-Century Employer Education Benefit

The Starbucks–ASU story began in 2013 with a meeting between Schultz and Crow at the Markle Foundation, where they were participants at a board of directors meeting. John and Mary R. Markle established their foundation in 1927 "to promote the advancement and diffusion of knowledge among people of the United States, and to promote the general good of mankind," (Markle, n.d., para. 1). The mission of Markle in the past century has evolved to its present-day focus on realizing the potential of information technology to address previously intractable public problems, for the health and future of all Americans (Markle, n.d.).

The shared mission of supporting the advancement of initiatives grounded in the spirit of Markle made it natural for Crow and Schultz to connect immediately over other intractable problems facing their organizations, the country, and the world. Crow and Schultz's brainchild of how to identify and deliver a comprehensive higher education benefit for Starbucks partners was developed through this initial meeting.

Laying the Foundation for a Groundbreaking Education Benefit

Starbucks leaders knew they wanted to provide something as ambitious as offering health care benefits to its part-time partners in 1987 while setting an example other companies should emulate in the present. Starbucks zeroed in on a goal to remove barriers for partners to earn a bachelor's degree. As leaders at Starbucks pushed to place higher education within reach, the company saw the potential of online higher education. Online degree programs appeared particularly well suited to working adults who already had some college experience but were impeded in obtaining a degree when life got in the way. Starbucks sought an education partner that offered high-quality online programs, ideally a nonprofit institution able to work at the scale necessary to serve Starbucks's large U.S. partner populations. This was a tall order as few education delivery partners had the qualifications necessary to make such a partnership successful.

The online higher education market had been dominated by for-profit online institutions, which was not a good fit for Starbucks. When Starbucks began searching for a higher education resource, most public and private universities had relatively few degree programs entirely online. Few institutions had the capability of offering online degree programs at a scale that could serve Starbucks's partners.

ASU, however, is a different kind of public university. It is constantly innovating and is committed to providing educational opportunities for learners at all levels by dedicating itself to developing the tools and resources traditional and nontraditional students need to be successful. As ASU has continued to grow and expand across the globe, the university developed methods to reach students at scale, integrated educational technologies, and moved quickly to improve its services to meet the needs of students wherever they are. ASU has used this approach to rapidly create online degree programs, which have grown from a handful of offerings at the undergraduate level to now more than 175 postsecondary and advanced degrees, all fully online (https://asuonline.asu.edu).

It all comes together under EdPlus, a central enterprise unit at ASU that grew out of the former online and extended campus portion of the university. EdPlus is focused on the design and scalable delivery of digital teaching and learning models to increase student success and reduce barriers to achievement in higher education. EdPlus advances the economic, social, cultural, and overall health of the local, national, and international communities served by ASU through more than 175 fully-online degree programs now benefitting more than 30,000 undergraduate and graduate students from Arizona, nationally and internationally, as well as students who are place-bound and those who benefit from a personalized style of learning. EdPlus also facilitates alternative degree pathways online for aspiring college students anywhere to improve and demonstrate university readiness and online continuing education for lifelong adult learners seeking professional development growth in their fields. EdPlus builds partnerships with universities and public and private corporations of all sizes to create customized digital learning education benefit programs; and EdPlus engages in deep learning analytics conducted by its in-house Action Lab, resulting in continuous program improvement and greater student achievement (Edplus.asu.edu).

Making an Online Higher Education Benefit Model Work

Starbucks leaders wanted to offer SCAP first in the United States, where there is the single largest concentration of partners. From the beginning, Starbucks and ASU identified common values. For Starbucks, it was ASU's focus and ability to provide high-quality education at scale, along with its willingness to work in partnership in innovating a new model of education access. It also valued ASU's personalized and focused attention on each of its students, a commitment now exemplified through the ASU Online Student Success Center. At ASU every online-degree-seeking student is paired with an ASU success coach, who is focused on ensuring that the student is successful from the first class through graduation (https://edplus.asu.edu/what-we-do/asu-online). Coaches answer questions ranging from how to sign up for the next term to what to do if a hurricane strikes a student's area and studies need to be paused.

ASU administrators recognized Starbucks's clear interest in providing its partners with a full undergraduate experience that promised no restrictions on employment or tuition repayment provisions following the completion of a degree. It became very apparent that Starbucks is as committed to its partners as ASU is to the welfare of its students and how they succeed at the university and beyond.

Soon after the Markle board meeting, senior leadership from Starbucks and ASU devised a strategy for a new kind of education benefit with a few key guidelines: minimal to no cost to partners; accessible education curriculum at scale, leading to a full university degree completed entirely online; and providing support to Starbucks partners along their education journey.

A senior strategist at Starbucks and the chief operating officer at EdPlus worked closely with leaders at each organization to flesh out the strategy and operational components necessary to implement what would become SCAP. Although the big idea may have been Schultz and Crow's, the practicalities of innovation required highly skilled leaders in the organizations to translate a vision into action. First, they established clear goals like making college affordable for middle-class workers and, second, allowed translation of these goals into measurable outcomes and objectives.

At ASU, major systems had to be overhauled to prepare for thousands of Starbucks partners to become ASU Online students. Because the initiative was driven from the top down at ASU, strong implementers inside ASU Online alongside senior leaders were essential to help lead innovation through other areas of the university such as admissions, student registrar, and financial aid. The cross-collaborations resulted in reduced time to decision on applications for students, increased accessibility to financial aid counselors and faster financial aid processes, and an accelerated review of transcripts for transfer students, all key changes that were implemented before the SCAP launch. These eventually affected all ASU students, online and on campus.

Ultimately, Starbucks rallies around its partners and customers the same way that ASU supports its students and community. The alignment of business values alongside people values allowed the teams to work together in less than one year to ideate, create, and launch SCAP.

Launching SCAP

On June 16, 2014, a group of partners at Starbucks and ASU leaders rang the NASDAQ Stock Market's opening bell to announce SCAP in what would be labeled as one of the greatest innovations in higher education to date (Solomon, 2015). As of publication, more than 2,300 Starbucks partners have graduated from ASU and nearly half are still employed by the company. Others have moved on to new roles outside the company, which Starbucks and ASU jointly celebrate.

Rapid Innovation Required

When SCAP was announced in June 2014, eligible partners enrolled as junior or senior students received full tuition reimbursement from Starbucks, and partners enrolled as freshmen or sophomores received a scholarship to assist with tuition coverage. It was clear almost immediately that a way to remove the financial burden for all partners, regardless of their year at the university, needed to be developed. ASU and Starbucks came together again to find a way to best reach all qualified partners, and in March 2015 they announced that SCAP would provide full tuition reimbursement for all enrolled partners ("Starbucks and ASU Offer Four Years of College with Full Tuition Coverage," 2015). This expansion allowed a major transformation again between Starbucks and ASU to provide even greater value to partners.

An additional expansion in February 2017 allowed partners not yet qualified for admission to the university to enter SCAP ("College Goals in Reach for Starbucks Partners, Thanks to 'Pathway,'" 2017). Real-time stories told to financial aid advisers and success coaches at ASU and feedback that store managers shared with their leadership led to the realization that a broader set of individuals wanted access to SCAP. Each month, about one-third of applicants to the university were being denied admission in large part because of their poor academic history.

Staff from the ASU's Office of the Provost, ASU Online, undergraduate admissions, and financial aid along with Starbucks's program leaders launched an inclusive modification to SCAP called Pathway to Admission offering Starbucks's partners a chance to earn admission to the university by taking rigorous course work delivered through ASU's Earned Admission program (https://ea.asu.edu). In less than a year, this new pathway for Starbucks's partners to achieve their college degrees generated more than 1,000 participating partners alone, and it continues to grow. In fact, it has been such a success that ASU has opened its earned admission program to any ASU Online prospective student who was previously denied admission.

Changing a program policy had taken months and months of legal alignment, and the design of a joint steering committee governing the program required an agreed-on process for making changes rapidly so that SCAP Pathway to Admissions could flourish. Fortunately, this process was in place between ASU and Starbucks and enabled the evolution of the program.

Congratulations, Graduates

Kaede Clifford was the first person to graduate from ASU through SCAP. Although Clifford was able to achieve this in a short time because of her previous college credits, SCAP allowed her to reach the goal of degree completion. By the end of 2018 SCAP supported more than 2,300 partners in achieving college degrees from all backgrounds, and more than 10,000 partners are actively participating in the program. By 2025 the program is anticipated to reach 25,000 graduates (Starbucks Coffee Company, 2018b). Undoubtedly, further innovation will be required to help move the program forward. Although expanding the program to include full tuition coverage for an undergraduate degree and pathways for those not yet eligible for admission to the university has been huge, other systems and processes will need to break new ground to accelerate the pace of innovation.

Key Lessons for Creating Sustainable Innovation

Intentional Collisions Lead to Transformation

Although the Markle Foundation brought Schultz and Crow to the same boardroom on the same day, there is something more to be said about the importance of networking. Schultz and Crow set the stage for a productive conversation leading to a framework of productive collaboration. For leaders in online education, no opportunity should be overlooked to exchange ideas, regardless of the different backgrounds individuals may be coming from such as a public university or a coffee shop. Often, great ideas arise from the least expected places. It may take two different mind-sets born of different industries colliding and ultimately working together to lead to transformation.

Find a Partner With a Shared Ethos

If your institution is looking to advance major initiatives at scale, the key is to find a partner with similar beliefs and philosophies, a shared ethos, and a challenge that both entities can tackle together. The size of a public company like Starbucks and the quick-moving, entrepreneurial motivation of Schultz to affect societal change, coupled with the drive, ingenuity, experience, and ability to scale ASU's operations and online programs under Crow's leadership provided a safe collaboration playground.

Establish a Nimble Infrastructure

A key lesson for leaders designing complex programs like SCAP is they must set up the right infrastructure to support open review, discussion, and decision-making to best advance the initiative. A diversity of decision makers outside one's own specialty is also key. As in the case of the steering committee comprising leaders from Starbucks and ASU ranging from human resources to public affairs to operations, it is essential to have all voices represented among major units that would be affected by a design change in the SCAP program.

Consider Investing in a Dedicated Partnership Acceleration Unit

The university's investment in a central services unit like EdPlus that constantly innovates to produce scalable systemic changes, works quickly, and whose administrators think differently are key ingredients of innovation, particularly with online education where trends and behaviors are rapidly changing and evolving. Such an investment can help accelerate new partnerships and programs for the university and become a good fit for a partner like Starbucks.

Strive for Parity of Degree Delivery

Given the complexity of most major universities—registrar systems, transcript evaluation processes, financial aid packaging, course enrollment—it is helpful to have a dedicated central team focused on online education delivery across all degree programs and colleges and academic units. ASU uniquely invests in employing the same faculty who teach campus immersion classes to teach digital immersion classes. Thus, the experience of a fully digital student at ASU is in parity with a campus immersion student because of the caliber and excellence of the faculty who are teaching the course work.

Work in the Current Design of the University

Try not to replicate functions and systems that exist for the entire university but rather work within the current design parameters of the university and adapt practices already in motion. For example, instead of duplicating a financial aid services team in ASU's EdPlus just for online students, the EdPlus team worked closely with central financial aid and student services to help develop a specialized team of advisers to discuss with Starbucks's student partners their unique benefit package and how financial aid would work for them. This ability to use a central university service while still developing specialized knowledge and functions of the central team is key to administrators who want to move quickly while taking advantage of the infrastructure already in place at their institution.

References

"Coffee czar: Executive chairman, former CEO, Starbucks." (2017). Retrieved from https://www.forbes.com/100-greatest-business-minds/person/howard-schultz

College goals in reach for Starbucks partners, thanks to "Pathway." (2017). Retrieved from https://news.starbucks.com/news/starbucks-pathway-to-admission-program

Crow, M. M. (2016, December 7). What being the first in my family to go to college taught me about opportunity. Retrieved from https://president.asu.edu/read/what-being-the-first-in-my-family-to-go-to-college-taught-me-about-opportunity

Markle. (n.d.). *About Markle*. Retrieved from https://www.markle.org/about-markle/

Number of Starbucks stores worldwide from 2003 to 2018. (2018). Retrieved on December 17, 2018, from https://www.statista.com/statistics/266465/number-of-starbucks-stores-worldwide/

Schultz, H. (1997). *Pour your heart into it: How Starbucks built a company one cup at a time*. New York, NY: Hyperion.

Solomon, M. (2015, October 25). Did Starbucks just create the most epic $250 million recruiting tool ever? *Forbes*. Retrieved from https://www.forbes.com/sites/micahsolomon/2015/10/24/did-starbucks-just-create-the-most-epic-250-million-recruitment-tool-ever/#7c9431497a5d

Starbucks and ASU offer four years of college with full tuition coverage. (2015, April 6). Retrieved from https://news.starbucks.com/news/starbucks-and-asu-expand-college-achievement-plan-full-tuition-coverage

Starbucks Coffee Company. (2018a). *Our mission*. Retrieved from http://www.starbucks.com/about-us/company-information/mission-statement

Starbucks Coffee Company. (2018b). *Starbucks CEO Kevin Johnson unveils innovation strategy to propel the company's next decade of growth at Starbucks 2018 annual meeting of shareholders*. Retrieved from https://investor.starbucks.com/press-releases/financial-releases/press-release-details/2018/Starbucks-ceo-Kevin-Johnson-Unveils-Innovation-Strategy-to-Propel-the-Companys-Next-Decade-of-Growth-at-Starbucks-2018-Annual-Meeting-of-Shareholders/default.aspx

7

ENSURING QUALITY WHILE CREATING AND INNOVATING

Deborah Adair and Kay Shattuck

The disruption to higher education caused by the emergence of online learning and the scope of its seemingly random implementation resulted rather quickly in calls for ensuring quality in online education even as institutions were creating and innovating. This is not a new phenomenon of change management, but it is rarely experienced at such a grand scale in education. A common understanding of quality in online education was sorely needed to support the development of effective online courses and to provide evidence to refute claims of inferiority of online education compared to face-to-face education. Creating such an understanding is a complex undertaking. *Quality standards* and *quality assurance* are terms that are batted around; however, it is crucial to understand the differences among (a) the articulation of the dimensions of quality, (b) the development of quality standards, and (c) the implementation of a quality assurance process. This chapter applies the lens of change management theory to quality assurance processes to frame a discussion of quality, quality standards, and quality assurance processes in online education.

Dimensions of Quality

Quality is an overarching construct that is a complex schema of the ideal and of excellence made up of characteristics or dimensions related to the final product. Relating that to online education, Mayadas (1997), working with the Alfred P. Sloan Foundation, founded the Asynchronous Learning Network (SLOAN-C ALN, reorganized in 2014 as the Online Learning Consortium) to provide grants and resources in support of establishing networks in higher education and training for anytime, anyplace learning and produced *The Five Pillars of Quality Online Education* (https://onlinelearningconsortium .org/about/quality-framework-five-pillars/). About the same time, Phipps and Merisotis (2000) produced *Quality on the Line: Benchmarks for Success in Internet-Based Distance Education.* Frydenberg (2002), Khan (2000), Lorenzo and Moore (2001), and Mariasingam and Hanna (2006) also developed well-received identifications of the domains of quality in online education. These listings of the dimensions of quality were themes identified by educational leaders at institutions with established online programs. For example, Phipps and Merisotis (2000) developed 7 benchmarking categories and 24 items that "institutions [should] strive to incorporate into their policies, practices, and procedures" to "ensure excellence in internet-based distance learning" (p. 1). In an effort to produce a framework for identification of the quality on online learning, the Council of Regional Accrediting Commissions (2011), developed *The Interregional Guidelines for the Evaluation of Distance Education* as guidance for higher education regional accrediting organization.

Specifying the dimensions of quality is the fundamental and entry-level part of every responsible innovation, initially to determine key commonalities among similar innovations and then to identify the factors supporting the most successful ones. This articulation of quality is the necessary beginning, but it is not sufficient for ensuring the continual development of quality standards or for their contextualized application. A focus on the outcomes of quality is a reasonable approach to new initiatives; however, sampling on the dependent variable (with success as the outcome) is not a robust way to isolate the determinants of success. It explains little, if anything, about the important contributing factors that lead to a successful outcome, how to replicate the outcome, or how to improve it. Research that adds rigor and removes bias in the determination of quality and identifies strong correlational or causal relationships must be the basis for developing quality standards. The effectiveness of such standards is dependent on inclusion of characteristics that can be tied to research and making them valid and useful in evaluating quality.

Development of Quality Standards

As the field of online learning has matured, the number of related quality standards and rubrics has increased. Today there are quality standards set for course, program, and institutional levels. In addition to the quality frameworks identified previously, rubrics for online quality are continuing to be developed. For example, the Online Learning Consortium Scorecard (Shelton, 2012) presented standards for online learning at an institutional level, and the Rubric for Online Instruction from California State University

(2018) and the Open SUNY Center Course Quality Review Rubric (2018) are standards that can be adapted by others. (See Adair, 2014, for information on additional rubrics.)

The International Boards of Standards for Training, Performance and Instruction (2018) provides standards backed by a regular, rigorous research process to "develop, validate, publish, and disseminate" performance statements, including instructors, training managers, instructional designers, and evaluators" (para. 2). Another example of quality standards for online learning backed by ongoing research comes from Quality Matters (QM, 2018). These standards are systematically researched every two to three years in a rigorous, transparent process that includes extensive review of the independent educational research, analysis of data collected from users, and a deep statistical analysis of data from previous QM peer reviews, as well as vetting by a team of online and QM experts (Shattuck, Zimmerman, & Adair, 2014).

QM (2018) is an international nonprofit organization providing a scalable quality assurance system for online and blended learning within and across organizations. It is used by more than 1,100 academic institutions to ensure quality in teaching and learning by providing the research-based and continuously informed definitions, tools, processes, and resources that support rigorous quality assurance processes. The QM processes are on a continuum that begins with the application of national and broadly accepted quality standards, moves to the introduction of a quality evaluation process, goes on to crafting a continuous improvement pathway, moves to an external benchmarking protocol, and culminates by institutionalizing and sustaining an organization's quality processes. QM's role is separate and distinct from that of an accreditor. QM is not the evaluation of the quality of an entire institution's operations, but it is focused squarely on the teaching- and learning-related functions in a framework to sustain new quality assurance practices over time.

Although describing what quality looks like and establishing standards for assessment is important work, ensuring quality is a completely separate endeavor. A quality assurance process is the way the hard work of creating effective quality standards is used to maintain, replicate, and improve the quality of an innovation. Implementation of such a process differs in terms of rigor and goals. For example, the dissemination of quality standards in an academic department or institution does not ensure quality nor does ad hoc implementation of quality standards.

Quality in Education

Traditionally, quality in higher education has been expressed in terms of the scholarly credentials of an institution's faculty, along with student acceptance patterns and rates (e.g., high school grade point average and College Board score), as well as the national ranking of the institution. This process-based approach has relied on input in the educational process with the assumption that if faculty and students are adequately prepared, a quality educational experience will result. Over the past several decades, however, a broader, external system of self-regulated regional accrediting bodies and professional credentialing programs has evolved and matured (Inglis, Ling, & Joosten, 1999; O'Brien, 2013). These accreditors led efforts to ensure continuous improvement, which has caught the eye of public funders of higher education. Julie Hamlin, executive director of MarylandOnline, who has served on a number of regional accreditation teams over the years, reflected about the current emphasis on accreditation:

> The accreditors want evidence, evidence, evidence—evidence of student learning achievement both during and after college. Course completion, course grades, grades on exams are not considered sufficient as evidence of student learning. Other means of measuring, sometimes supplied by outside vendors, are encouraged. . . . Accreditors also want evidence that institutions are *using* the results of SLO [student learning outcomes] assessment to improve teaching, curriculum, et cetera. (J. Hamlin, personal communication, December 17, 2016)

Although the emphasis continues to be on continuous improvement processes, regional accreditors are increasingly looking for evidence in terms of outcomes and, in particular, in student learning.

Enter Online Education: Creating and Innovating Quality Assurance

Online education arrived on the higher education scene through a number of avenues. In some cases, it was prompted by a continuation of decades or even a century of a focus on adult learners at small distance education programs at land-grant institutions, and a natural evolutionary next phase that broadcast forms of distance education (courses delivered by television). In other cases, it happened through a quick, jump-on-the-bandwagon administrative reaction. Often, online education sprang from a grassroots movement by a small group of faculty who had explored adding Internet technologies to their own courses; in other cases, it came about after strategic discussion and planning at an organizational level (Chaloux & Miller, 2014). In whatever way online education became part of an educational organization, it is safe to say that it was accompanied by a call for ensuring quality of online learning. Christensen (2018) and others (Anderson, 2008; Meyer, 2010) have written extensively about the ways technology disrupted higher education, bringing along with it an influx of adult learners and interactivity possibilities. This disruption led some educators to change emphasis from content provision or delivery to student learning by active learning as an all-important outcome. As Hanna (2013) stated,

> Learning opportunities begin with the needs of the learner rather than the specific knowledge to be conveyed by the teacher. . . . Transformational change involves changing the nature of the work of the university, reorienting its purpose, and refocusing its intent, and involves deep changes in the culture of the organization.
>
> As demand for higher education has increased globally, universities are operating in a more competitive and business-like environment than ever before. New technologies are both enabling and forcing changes in learning and teaching. . . . In many cases, [online] distance learning is the driver for providing leadership for implementing new ideas, approaches, and models and for leading organizational change within residential universities. (pp. 691–693)

The learning outcomes movement, which started in undergraduate education in the 1970s, intensified with online education, along with other concerns that online was equivalent to traditional, classroom-based learning formats. The increased call for evidence of outcomes that parallels the growth of online education is essentially a call for recalibration of processes to ensure quality. Increasing the transparency of outcomes provides the opportunity to reexamine the definitions and determinants of quality and to think critically about the rigor of processes. The development of meaningful quality standards and their application in a quality assurance process is the mechanism to move from the accomplishment of a single, successful innovation, defined by outcomes achieved, to make the organizational changes necessary to replicate and extend those positive outcomes over time. For innovations to evolve into actual, sustained institutional change, the focus needs to build first from new definitions of quality, next to create specific criteria or standards, and finally to a rigorous quality assurance process that provides continuous feedback that encourages and supports organizational learning.

Implementation of a Quality Assurance Process

Quality assurance is the fundamental learning tool for organizations to innovate and change. Creating and innovating, in an organization at least, is not an end in itself. The purpose is to change the organization in strategic, positive, and productive ways; to identify what works; and to learn from what works to improve and achieve results. Thus, organizational learning is a fundamental aspect of the organizational change required for an innovation to be sustainable and impactful. Organizations that succeed in implementing and sustaining innovation are learning organizations that engage in what Argyris (1976) has termed *single-loop* and *double-loop learning*. Organization leaders who want to be successful in sustaining their innovations need to regularly evaluate when and how to make appropriate corrections in their implementation (single-loop learning) and to understand when and how to modify models, policies, and even the objectives of the innovation (double-loop learning). Garvin (1993) further explained the value of organization in developing skills in "systematic problem-solving, experimentation, learning from their own and others' experiences and transferring knowledge" (para. 14). In essence, successful innovations require the kind of organizational learning that is captured in meaningful quality assurance processes that reflect an organization's capacity for systematic problem-solving and benchmarking (comparing processes and performance outcomes) in and outside the organization. Rather than stifling innovation with prescriptive and rigid processes, quality assurance is fundamental to the successful dissemination of innovations.

Maturing of an Innovation

The structure and implementation of quality assurance processes can vary in scope and rigor. Different levels of implementation excellence in a quality assurance process follow the maturation. A model for improving the implementation of quality assurances practices in online education has been developed by Adair, reflecting more than 10 years of observation and practice of QM implementation, data analysis, and validation from the field (see www .qualitymatters.org/qa-resources/resource-center/conference-presentations/ qms-qa-continuum-excellence-where-are-you-and). This model is, not surprisingly, similar to other process improvement models such as the Capability Maturity Model Integration created for software development processes by Carnegie Mellon University (see https://en.wikipedia.org/wiki/Capability_ Maturity_Model_Integration for basic information). In the early stage of an innovation, the quality assurance effort is focused on the identification and introduction of quality criteria. As the leaders of an organization learn more about quality dimensions, they can begin to introduce and apply the criteria to their processes as they experiment and problem solve (QA Level 1). With a firm set of criteria, organizations can then build a customized and differentiated application of the criteria to evaluate the innovation in its current state and refine actions and behaviors (QA Level 2). It can move from such single-loop learning to a continuous improvement process that broadens the feedback and its application to begin to accommodate double-loop learning

(QA Level 3). To increase the openness of the quality assurance system and to be able to evaluate its experiences in relationship to others, the quality assurance process needs to include benchmarking or comparisons across organizations to develop and act on a shared understanding of quality (QA Level 4). Finally, excellence in the implementation of the quality assurance process is achieved when the innovation and its quality assurance process are institutionalized in ways that support and sustain the changes over time (QA Level 5). An effective implementation of a quality assurance process starts by specifically defining what is meant by *quality*. What is it, exactly, that needs to be ensured and advanced? Criteria need to be identified in a particular context and commonly understood or agreed on. Then criteria should be applied in replicable, systematic ways. (This model is further explained in the Implementation of a Quality Assurance Process section of this chapter).

Development of Quality Standards

The creation of quality standards is critical. Attention needs to be paid to the characteristics of the standards, that is, they have a well-defined scope and are measurable, meaningful, relevant, transparent, and current. From a practical perspective, defining the scope of application is a critical step. Edges or boundaries to what the criteria do and do not apply to and what will and will not be evaluated are required, otherwise quality assurance becomes an endless pursuit. The standards have to be measurable—practically and reliably—to guide positive action. Quality standards need to be meaningful and relevant for the community engaged in their application and for the stakeholders of that effort. The standards have to be transparent to ensure they are commonly understood, even though training is likely required for consistent application. Also, they must be kept current; the commitment to reevaluate the criteria as well as their performance is a part of the double-loop learning that supports successful organizational change. Creating effective quality standards, however, is limited to an interesting exercise if the criteria are not then activated through a rigorous quality assurance process.

Implementation of a Quality Assurance Process

Establishing quality definitions and standards is only impactful when included in a doable quality assurance process that can be implemented in an organization. Implementation is not a uniform effort but a complex dynamic that is expressed in five levels of measurable action in the institution (see Figure 7.1): an ad hoc approach, a quality assurance evaluation, a continuous improvement process, benchmarking for comparison and transparency,

Figure 7.1.   Continuum of excellence in quality assurance.

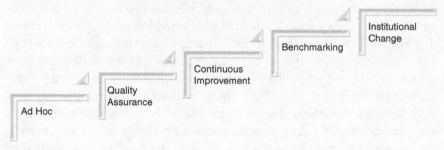

and systemic institutional change. Examples are provided from institutional implementation of QM.

QA Level 1: An Ad Hoc Approach

The ad hoc approach to quality assurance implementation can be categorized as voluntary or episodic, nonsystematic, and nonstrategic. In this stage, individuals involved in the innovation familiarize themselves with the quality standards and learn how they work. The goal is to start empowering people to understand and use the criteria and related resources to informally evaluate quality as the innovation moves forward. A quality assurance process is not mandated by the organization, nor is the use of quality criteria systematic. The benefits to such an approach in the early stages of an innovation are clear. It offers a low-stakes way to start the quality assurance process that is nonthreatening to constituents with minimal investments in staff time, money, and other resources. This approach can provide the time for individuals to become familiar with the quality standards and for early adopters to begin to use them to guide their efforts and showcase their success. This approach might be particularly relevant for fledgling innovations that are difficult to communicate or that may be initially controversial.

However, the ad hoc approach makes it difficult to develop momentum for ongoing implementation, especially if there is minimal institutional awareness of the effort. With no specific or articulated processes in place, there is little in the initiative that can be taken to scale, that is adaptable to institutions with differing and growing needs. Fundamentally, the ad hoc approach provides exposure to quality standards but does not address needs for quality assurance of the innovation and does not achieve even single-loop learning with any consistency or scale.

Academic institutions that take into account the need for quality assurance as they begin or expand their online activities are a case in point. In these cases, institutions will create or adopt a rubric, such as the QM Rubric (www.qualitymatters.org/qa-resources/rubric-standards), to guide their course development and to identify a desirable standard of quality for their community. They may use this rubric to guide collaboration between instructional designers and subject matter experts, create course design templates for voluntary adoption and use by faculty, and encourage faculty to self-review using the tool. The initial implementation of the QM framework is often ad hoc in this way for a number of reasons. Campus faculty may be new to online education and find a requirement to develop their courses to meet such a robust set of quality standards daunting or even threatening. A college may need time to educate key stakeholders on the need for a set of external standards and to understand what kind of quality review process makes sense for its culture, capacity, and budget. An ad hoc approach allows the time and space that is needed to prepare the organization and key stakeholders for the implementation of the QM process, something that most change management theorists have identified as essential for a successful organizational change. See Kaminski's (2011), description of Lewin's three-step change theory or Kotter's (1996) eight-stage process.

QA Level 2: A Quality Evaluation

The purpose of the quality evaluation approach is to put in place an unbiased, rigorous process to evaluate and report (internally) on the state of quality of the innovation. The focus is on ensuring that components of the innovation are meeting an equivalent level of quality, based at least in part on best practice standards. However, the quality criteria and process are often highly customized to the specific organization and the units involved in the innovation. Garvin, Edmondson, and Gino (2008) noted the importance of understanding and reflecting local cultures of learning and the way norms and behavior vary across units within organizations. Because the learning maturity of the units varies, the quality assurance criteria and processes tend to be customized to meet the specific learning culture of the units engaged in the innovation.

At this stage, quality assurance is about setting a bar and ensuring it is met. It is not about scalability, continuous improvement processes, or long-term learning or growth. This implementation of a quality evaluation process represents effective single-loop learning; however, it is unlikely to be sustainable long term as the innovation evolves and expands.

This quality evaluation process is a goal for most academic institutions involved with QM. It is a significant achievement to successfully overcome initial resistance to a rigorous quality framework, to implement a consistent process to quality check an identified set of courses over a specific time frame, and to act on the results of the review. For these institutions, the quality assurance process is typically customized to address specific points of resistance or to enable a quicker start-up and may not reflect the full set of quality standards or full process promoted by QM. It is often implemented in specific campus academic departments and managed by a centralized unit with responsibility for quality in online teaching and learning, faculty development, or course design. The review in these quality assurance processes is usually conducted by a relatively small number of individuals to provide a check after course development but before a course is delivered. Institutions typically develop a cycle for rereview of courses based on the rubric standards every few years. The importance of savvy customization at this stage, consistent with management strategies for implementing organizational change (Kotter, 1996), is that it allows short-term wins and establishes a proof of concept of what can be achieved on a broader or more rigorous scale going forward. As the number of online courses to be reviewed or rereviewed increases, institutions need to look for a more scalable process that can inform their course design and development efforts in manageable and efficient ways.

QA Level 3: A Continuous Improvement Process

The continuous improvement approach builds on but goes beyond implementation of a quality evaluation process. It involves a regular and ongoing process of review using a consistent application of criteria and includes policies and processes for action, feedback, and revision. The broader feedback loop and application of results require broader participation across the organization in a way that perpetuates and extends the use of the quality standards and evaluation beyond the initial review. This provides an internal measure of quality assurance and can establish a scalable continuous improvement process for the innovation. It represents double-loop learning when the use of the review results goes beyond evaluating the success of the innovation to reevaluate the criteria as well as the assumptions about how the innovation can and should affect the organization (and vice versa). This ongoing experimentation with the application of quality standards and the results of the review engages a greater number of organizational members in the evaluation of quality, broadening the process and its reach.

Academic institutions seeking an efficient way to scale the involvement and impact of the implementation of the QM process will develop a continuous improvement process that uses many of their own faculty members in the review of their courses. These faculty members provide the quality check for the courses they review and offer detailed feedback that can help the courses continue to improve over time. In addition, the engagement in course review motivates the reviewers to apply the standards to improve their own courses as well. QM has collected data over the past 10 years (2006–2016) that support the exponential effect of using teaching faculty as course reviewers (Adair, 2014). A single review involves 3 reviewers and the course developer, each indicating they make improvements to their own courses as a result of their experience on a single review panel. Assuming each faculty member makes changes to just 3 courses each year, and that each teaches an average of 30 students per course, a single course review using this protocol could positively affect the learning environment for 360 students. In addition, anecdotal evidence suggests that as the critical mass of individuals involved in this continuous improvement process increases, the ideas for extending the application of the quality standards to other teaching modalities and institutional teaching policies have also increased.

Institutions using the QM (Adair, 2014; Shattuck, Zimmerman, & Adair, 2014) tools and processes (www.qualitymatters.org/qa-resources/rubric-standards) in a continuous improvement process can track and report on commonalities and trends based on their course review data. Examining review results over time, and evaluating trends in the feedback provided in review reports, administrators can determine areas of strengths and weaknesses in their institutional design and development processes, which provide direction about institutional processes and protocols. Committees with a focus on quality in online education are able to consider broader implications of the quality standards used in the review process. Often, institutional policy discussions regarding many aspects of online teaching and learning are a result. A broadly shared understanding of quality provides a platform for experimentation about quality beyond course design. Consistent with the seventh stage in Kotter's (1996) model for successful organizational change, the gains from the course review process are recognized, and the extension of the standards and protocols to other areas produces more positive change.

QA Level 4: Benchmarking for Comparison and Transparency

This level combines the continuous improvement processes, which have been customized to meet the culture and norms of the organization with results based on internal evaluation, with an external benchmarking process to ensure rigor, avoid bias, and make meaning from one's own experience in comparison with others. To understand the soundness of the quality assurance process and the quality of the innovation, organizations need a way to compare processes and results with relevant others. Garvin and colleagues (2008) explained that "comparative performance is the critical scorecard" (p. 8) and suggested that scoring high in a self-evaluation does not mean the process or outcomes identified will be a source of competitive advantage. What is more important, in terms of critical learning attributes, is how the organization compares with relevant others or to benchmark data. Excellence in quality assurance includes the benchmarking process and performance. Leaders who want their organizations to be successful in sustaining their innovations must be able to learn from their experience relative to that of others.

The QM's certification mark is earned by institutions and organizations that have met a specific evaluation threshold in the application of the entire set of QM standards and have used a review team and process that adheres to specific, rigorous review protocols (Adair, 2014; Shattuck, Zimmerman, & Adair, 2014). The certification mark on a course signifies that the course officially met QM Standards by being evaluated against the same set of standards in the same manner. Some academic institutions have a goal to achieve certification for all their courses; others have a plan to achieve certification of a representative number of courses across specific programs or disciplines as a benchmark for comparison and transparency. Such benchmarking activities help demonstrate the quality equivalency with their customized review processes and also allow the institution leaders to learn from a broader, more diverse set of reviewers than they can find in their own institution.

QA Level 5: Systemic Institutional Change

To create systemic institutional change, an organization needs to master the single- and double-loop learning represented in the previous QA levels as well as engage in benchmarking processes and outcomes. In addition, it needs to embed successful processes in ways that integrate with the institution's mission and strategic plans, align with its rewards systems, commit resources, and—perhaps most important—share and integrate knowledge. This is about the organizational change necessary to sustain and extend the innovation over time. Such efforts should provide the framework that raises broader questions about quality and engages the institution in conversation about continuing changes necessary to improve outcomes. What's required, as Kotter (1996) phrases it, is to "anchor new approaches in the culture" (p. 145).

Ultimately, organizations that want to move their innovation from a pilot, limited application, or ad hoc approach to a fully integrated and supported implementation to institutionalize the changes as standard operating procedures need to institutionalize the quality assurance process as well. Particularly in regard to innovation, *quality assurance approaches* (defined by continuous improvement, benchmarking performance, and a systemic approach to change) are a fundamental part of any sustainability effort.

According to Kotter (1996), anchoring the change requires modifying the institutional infrastructure, including people, to recognize and support the validity of the new quality practices. The culture change required to fully embrace and embed the changes comes at the end of the process. In this way, robust quality practices that support an innovation simply become business as usual.

Discussion

The reason many innovations never succeed is because changing an organization is exceedingly difficult, especially in organizations with strong cultural traditions such as those in higher education. Online learning formats entered education primarily as a disruptive invasion to tradition. As such, they challenged—for the whole institutional organization—what a quality education means and how the outcomes are to be measured and presented to the various shareholders. Ensuring the quality of an innovation is, in essence, a change initiative for the organization that can be expressed on a continuum, or stages, of excellence, that begins with understanding and introducing quality criteria, moves through development of quality standards, and arrives at the goal of sustaining the changes and demonstrating positive outcomes over time. Academic institutions are no different from other organizations when it comes to implementing the changes required to support a quality online innovation. They should be able to follow a pathway to excellence that makes sense for their mission and realities, helps them learn and improve, benchmarks their processes and achievements with relevant others, and drives them to a place where they can support and sustain an approach to innovation and change that best serves their learners. For these institutions, effectively navigating the stages in implementing change (successfully performing at the last step on the continuum) is what ensures a quality online experience for their learners.

Online education, and the many other innovations that have sprung from it, require organizational leaders and educators to think carefully about the maturity of their innovations and their institution's capacity for organizational learning. Are there research-based definitions of *quality* and carefully constructed criteria that can be applied to evaluate the innovation? If not, can the institution contribute to the development of such standards? If such standards exist, how prepared is the institution to implement a quality assurance process to maintain, improve, and extend the innovation? Skilled leadership is required to move successfully through the stages of a change initiative. It is important to know when the conditions are appropriate for the development of a quality assurance process and then determine where to begin its implementation. Similar to the prevailing wisdom in working with learners, skilled leaders of online learning innovations meet the institution and its stakeholders where they are in terms of quality processes and plan carefully a stepwise process of leading the institutions through the various stages of quality assurance until it is embedded in and defines the practice of online education. As cautioned by Deming, "It does not happen all at once. There is no instant pudding" (as cited by Bellows, 2017, para. 7). Quality, then, is the habit formed from the effort and practice involved in the process of ensuring excellence in innovation and change.

Summary

Online learning has been an innovation in education over the past several decades that raised the discussion of ensuring quality and a call to include evidence of outcomes. The call is essentially for the recalibration of processes to make quality criteria relevant for online learning innovations, which has been expanded on in this chapter using an organizational learning framework with the distinction of defining the dimensions of quality, the development of quality standards, and the implementation of a quality assurance process. Five levels of implementation of quality assurance processes were introduced to evolve innovations and grow them into actual, sustained institutional change.

References

Adair, D. (2014). A process to improve course design: A key variable in course quality. In K. Shattuck (Ed.), *Assuring quality in online education: Practices and processes at teaching, resource, and program levels* (pp. 81–90). Sterling, VA: Stylus.

Anderson, T. (2008, June 26). Disruptive, online education to go main stream [Web log post]. Retrieved from http://terrya.edublogs.org/2008/06/26/disruptive -online-education-to-go-main-stream/

Argyris, C. (1976). Single-loop and double-loop methods in research on decision making. *Administrative Science Quarterly, 21*, 363–375. doi:10.2307/2391848 .JSTOR 2391848

Bellows, B. (2017, November 27). Instant karma! And instant pudding [Web log post]. Retrieved from https://blog.deming.org/2017/11/instant-karma-and-instant-pudding/

California State University. (2018). *Rubric for online instruction (ROI)*. Retrieved from https://www.csuchico.edu/eoi/

Capability Maturity Model Integration. (2018). *About CCMIR Institute*. Retrieved from https://cmmiinstitute.com/company

Chaloux, B., & Miller, G. (2014). The impact of organizational context. In G. Miller, M. Benke, B. Chaloux, L. Ragan, R. Schroeder, W. Smutz., & K. Swan (Eds.). *Leading the e-learning transformation of higher education: Meeting the challenges of technology and distance education* (pp. 23–37). Sterling, VA: Stylus.

Christensen, C. M. (2018). *Disruptive innovation*. Retrieved from https://www.christenseninstitute.org/disruptive-innovations/

Council of Regional Accreditation Commissions. (2011). *Interregional guidelines for the evaluation of distance education*. Retrieved from http://nc-sara.org/files/docs/C-RAC%20Guidelines.pdf

Frydenberg, J. (2002). Quality standards in e-learning: A matrix of analysis. *International Review of Research in Open and Distance Learning, 3*(2), 1–15. Retrieved from http://www.irrodl.org/index.php/irrodl/article/view/109/189

Garvin, D. A. (1993). Building a learning organization. *Harvard Business Review, 71*(4): 78–91. Retrieved from https://hbr.org/1993/07/building-a-learning-organization

Garvin, D. A., Edmondson, A. C., & Gino, F. (2008, March). Is yours a learning organization? *Harvard Business Review*. Retrieved from https://hbr.org/2008/03/is-yours-a-learning-organization

Hanna, D. E. (2013). Emerging organizational models in higher education. In M. G. Moore (Ed.), *Handbook of distance education* (3rd ed., pp. 684–694). New York, NY: Routledge.

Inglis, A., Ling, P., & Joosten, V. (1999). *Delivering digitally: Managing the transition to the knowledge media*. London, UK: Kogan Page.

International Board of Standards for Training, Performance and Instruction. (2018). *Competency sets*. Retrieved from http://ibstpi.org/about-us/

Kaminski, J. (2011). Theory applied to informatics: Lewin's change theory. *CJNI: Canadian Journal of Nursing Informatics, 6*(1). Retrieved from http://cjni.net/journal/?p=1210

Khan, B. H. (2000). A framework for Web-based learning. *Tech Trends, 44*(3), 51. doi:10.1007/BF02778228

Kotter, J. P. (1996). *Leading change*. Boston, MA: Harvard Business School Press.

Lorenzo, G., & Moore, J. (2002, November). *The Sloan Consortium report to the nation: Five pillars of quality online education*. Retrieved from https://www.immagic.com/eLibrary/ARCHIVES/GENERAL/SLOANCUS/S021106L.pdf

Mariasingam, M. A., & Hanna, D. E. (2006). Benchmarking quality in online degree programs status and prospects. *Online Journal of Distance Learning Administration, 9*(3). Retrieved from http://www.westga.edu/~distance/ojdla/fall93/mariasingam93.htm

Mayadas, F. (1997). Asynchronous learning networks: A Sloan Foundation perspective. Retrieved from https://onlinelearningconsortium.org/sites/default/files/v1n1_mayadas_1.pdf

Meyer, K. (2010, March 3). The role of disruptive technology in the future of higher education. *EDUCAUSE Review*. Retrieved from http://er.educause.edu/articles/2010/3/the-role-of-disruptive-technology-in-the-future-of-higher-education

O'Brien, P. M. (2013). Accreditation: Assuring quality and fostering improvement. In M. G. Moore (Ed.), *Handbook of distance education* (3rd ed., pp. 481–492). New York, NY: Routledge.

Online Learning Consortium. (2018). The five pillars of quality online education. Retrieved from https://onlinelearningconsortium.org/about/quality-framework-five-pillars/

Open SUNY Course Quality Review Rubric. (2018). Retrieved from https://oscqr.org/

Phipps, R., & Merisotis, J. (2000). *Quality on the line: Benchmarks for success in Internet-based distance education*. Retrieved from http://www.ihep.org/sites/default/files/uploads/docs/pubs/qualityontheline.pdf

Quality Matters. (2018). *Quality assurance begins with a set of standards*. Retrieved from https://www.qualitymatters.org/qa-resources/rubric-standards

Shattuck, K., Zimmerman, W. A., & Adair, D. (2014). Continuous improvement of the QM rubric and review processes: scholarship of integration and application. *Internet Learning, 3*(1), 25–34.

Shelton, K. (2012). *A quality scorecard for the administration of online education programs: A Delphi study.* Retrieved from https://www.researchgate.net/publication/228384041_A_Quality_Scorecard_for_the_Administration_of_Online_Education_Programs_A_Delphi_Study

8

SUPPORTING CREATIVITY AND INNOVATION THROUGH PROFESSIONAL DEVELOPMENT AND COMMUNITY BUILDING

Jill Buban, Cali M.K. Morrison, Karen L. Pedersen,
Amy Claire Heitzman, and Julie Uranis

N ow more than ever, higher education professionals are being called on to drive innovation and implement innovative practices on their campuses. In an era when presentations focusing on mixed reality are becoming mainstream at educational technology conferences, competency-based education initiatives are being launched at institutions, various forms of alternative credentials are being recognized by employers and institutions alike, and promising adaptive learning solutions are providing more personalized learning environments, higher education professionals find themselves in a dynamic and changing landscape. As the rate of implementation for these innovations increases, so does the need for higher education professionals to have a community to interact with others in the digital learning ecosystem. Whether for administrators or other campus leaders, faculty members, instruction or learning designers, or student service professionals, formal and informal communities provide a space to share ideas and experiences, receive feedback, and learn from peers.

This chapter provides an overview of three organizations that offer opportunities for modern digital learning professionals to build their community and develop professionally as digital learning becomes ever more ubiquitous. The three formal communities are the Online Learning Consortium (OLC), the University Professional Continuing Education

Association (UPCEA), and the Western Interstate Commission for Higher Education (WICHE) Cooperative for Educational Technologies (WCET). Each organization provides a plethora of resources and solutions to support creativity and innovation through professional development and community building.

Following the overview of these formal communities and their resources, we explore several informal communities, many of which may sustain themselves over months or years, whereas other informal communities may be more organic communities designed to tackle a specific issue, trend, or opportunity.

Early Days of Professional Development for Online Leaders

In 1991, the Alfred P. Sloan Foundation funded the Anytime, Anyplace Learning program to better understand and develop programs that serve higher education students who could not attend courses on campus (e.g., students who required distance education or asynchronous learning) (Picciano, 2013). The program quickly became known as the Asynchronous Learning Network and allowed educators and learners to "transcend time and space" (p. i). This was the beginning of the community that formed to learn how the Internet could serve learners, which evolved into the Sloan Foundation and formed much of its work around the Sloan Consortium (Sloan-C) Five Pillars of Quality Online Education: access, faculty satisfaction, learning effectiveness, student satisfaction, and scale (OLC, 2017). Now simply referred to as the five pillars, the Sloan Foundation's work is one of the earliest examples of quality standards relevant to online education. The fact that they are still widely used today across the United States and internationally further legitimatizes the practices contained in the five pillars.

The Sloan-Community held its first annual conference 25 years ago in Orlando, Florida. The conference has grown significantly and convenes each fall. In 2014 the Sloan Consortium made the transition to the not-for-profit Online Learning Consortium (OLC, 2017). As the field evolved, so did the consortium; however, it remains the largest digital learning community, convening thousands of people annually and serving educators in a variety of ways. Additional long-standing formal communities have also been created, including UPCEA and WCET. These three organizations uniquely serve the digital learning field and collaborate to best serve the field holistically. With their unique and common attributes, the organizations are well situated to assist higher education professionals in better understanding, improved decision-making for, and implementation of innovations on their campuses.

Organizations for Online Learning Professionals

The work the Sloan Foundation supported many years ago continues to evolve. Other organizations with their own unique histories have contributed formal learning communities to support the work of online professionals, namely, UPCEA and WCET. The UPCEA and WCET have a rich history of engaging professionals who support online teaching and learning through focused entities such as the National Center for Online Education (NCOE), powered by UPCEA and WCET. In the following, we discuss these three organizations and their contributions to the professional development needs of online professionals.

OLC

The OLC is devoted to advancing quality online and blended learning by providing professional development, instruction, research and best practice publications, and guidance to educators, online learning professionals, and organizations around the world. The OLC is a key factor in the transformation of the digital learning field. Through conferences, quality learning opportunities, research initiatives, and tools and resources for individual and institutional success, the OLC has been an active part of the swift growth that has occurred in the field.

The OLC's vast array of resources are available anytime and anywhere because the organization recognizes that faculty, instructional designers, and administrators worldwide are looking for training, research, and quality measures in a timely manner. The OLC offers research and publications including a peer-reviewed academic journal, face-to-face and online professional development opportunities, a suite of quality scorecards, and a vast array of awards for community demonstrations of innovative practices.

Research and publications on research studies, case studies, white papers, and books in the field keep professionals informed as technology is radically changing how teaching and learning are approached. The OLC launched the Research Center for Digital Learning and Leadership (https://online learningconsortium.org/read/olc-research-center-digital-learning-leadership/) in 2017, and through collaborations with organizations and higher education institutions, the OLC conducts as well as curates research and makes it available as an open resource to all. Areas of focus include digital learning leadership, teaching and learning, instructional and learning design, digital courseware, quality, learning analytics, credentials, and resources focused on the adult learner.

The *Online Learning Journal* (formerly *Journal of Asynchronous Learning Networks*) is the OLC's peer-reviewed journal. Published quarterly, the journal has been in publication for two decades and often includes special issues focused on timely topics pertinent to the field. The journal's aim is to promote the development and dissemination of new knowledge at the intersection of pedagogy, emerging technology, policy, and practice in online environments. The journal provides a community for those in the field to convene around common areas of interest through its biannual conference panels, as well as through its collaboration with the American Education Research Association in which the Online Teaching and Learning Special Interest Group and the *Online Learning Journal* collaborate to offer information to scholars in the field.

Although scholarly development is of interest to one segment of the digital learning community, there is also interest in professional development opportunities including just-in-time learning; networking at conferences; and peer-to-peer learning through conference, webinar, and podcast offerings. For more than 10 years, the OLC Institute for Professional Development has offered educational and professional development opportunities in online teaching and learning through online workshops, multiple mastery series, and certificate programs. The schedule of offerings is published annually and updated on a regular basis as innovative topics and directions emerge. Self-paced courses were added in 2017. The institute offers a wide range of programs for those interested in deepening pedagogical and practitioner aspects of their teaching practice.

OLC webinars and podcasts provide an opportunity for professionals to learn about topics that are pertinent to current initiatives at their institutions. Webinars feature thought leaders from around the world discussing a wide array of topics and most recently featured a series on digital scholarship, a series on learning analytics, digital content curation, artificial intelligence, and online science labs. The OLC also shares industry-related podcasts on the organization's website including University of Central Florida's TOPcast (https://cdl.ucf.edu/teach/resources/topcast/), Oregon State University's Research in Action (https://ecampus.oregonstate.edu/podcast), and EdSurge On Air (www.edsurge.com/news/community/edsurge-podcast).

OLC conferences have also provided a place for digital learning professionals to convene and learn for the past 25 years. The OLC Accelerate and OLC Innovate annual conferences host thousands of people in person and virtually. Additionally, the OLC provides 1-day events called OLC Collaborates, cohosted by institutions around the country. These regional events bring speakers and participants together for a day of collaboration and engagement.

The Leadership Network and the Institute for Emerging Leadership in Online Learning are opportunities for leaders to network with peers and learn about topics pertinent to leaders in digital learning. The Leadership Network convenes twice a year at OLC conferences, whereas the institute is an immersive blended learning opportunity that includes an online primer, a four-day face-to-face immersion experience, and a postimmersion project component culminating in a master's class held in conjunction with OLC's Accelerate conference.

Finally, building on the early foundations of the five pillars, the OLC has developed a Suite of Quality Scorecards (https://onlinelearningconsortium .org/consult/olc-quality-scorecard-suite/). The growing suite of scorecards, which are freely available for download, offer easy-to-use tools for administrators, instructional designers, and faculty members. The tools are applicable at the course and program levels, and at the institutional level depending on deployment. The reason for implementation varies depending on use and can include a focus on continuous improvement, how to differentiate from competitors, and advance preparation for an accreditation review.

UPCEA

UPCEA is the leading association for professional, continuing, and online education. Founded in 1915, UPCEA is a member-driven nonprofit association of many of the leading public and private colleges and universities in North America. For more than 100 years, the association has served its members with innovative conferences and specialty seminars, research and benchmarking information, professional networking opportunities, and timely publications. Based in Washington DC, UPCEA also builds greater awareness of the vital link between contemporary learners and public policy issues. As the leading organization committed to advancing the adult learner, UPCEA's long history balances the complementary domains most germane to adult student access and success: professional and continuing education and online leadership.

These domains are complementary because of the relationship between professional and continuing education and online education. As noted by Kentor (2015), online learning is rooted in distance education, specifically the correspondence education movement of the eighteenth century. What began as vocationally focused learning efforts evolved into divisions of continuing a professional education or extended learning—the very same units often charged with leading online learning enterprises at colleges and universities today. UPCEA provides events and resources that inform the leadership and strategic direction of online enterprises, situating this work in the community of those who serve adult and nontraditional learners as the knowledge, skills, and attitudes needed to serve these learners are often similar to, or the same as, those needed to support online learners. UPCEA's professional development is focused on providing critical resources for the staff and faculty engaged in work that is increasingly mainstream, acute, and integral to institutional success.

In terms of knowledge dissemination, UPCEA produces an online journal, *Unbound*, which explores higher education issues through the lens of adult learners. This digital publication frequently highlights best and emerging practices in online education to support the learning of online professionals. The important trends and innovations published in *Unbound* inform the work of online professionals and leaders in educational technology companies. This publication, when paired with briefings, digital newsletters, and social media, supports a comprehensive communication strategy that serves the information needs of online professionals.

Serving the adult learner is rarely a one-size-fits-all approach and no two campuses address these varied needs in the same way. Compared to the OLC's structured learning programs, UPCEA involves professionals seeking to develop their personal leadership capacity through engagement and leading peers. UPCEA's major volunteer structures—regions and networks—are responsive, dynamic, member-driven bodies designed to offer multiple points of access that members can tailor to the unique demands of their personal professional development needs as well as the needs of their institutions.

UPCEA's five regions provide opportunities for members to examine issues of local and regional importance, develop collaborative initiatives, and network with area colleagues. The economies of geography also furnish cost-effective ways for new and midlevel staff to participate in regional conferences, whether individually or as a team. UPCEA's six networks are designed to serve midlevel to more senior professionals across the organization practicing in the key areas that define this vibrant and growing sector of higher education. As a professional home for members who work in an area of practice, each network provides opportunities for like-minded members to meet and collaborate on a variety of deliverables, from conference content to webinars to research and scholarship, all while growing as a professional among peers.

The Online Administration Network is the professional home for all levels of online leaders. This focused network recognizes strategic innovations in online education by presenting the Strategic Innovation in Online Education

Award, which offers leaders an opportunity to shine a spotlight on the work being done at their institution and an additional professional development opportunity in the form of a conference presentation at the UPCEA's annual conference.

UPCEA has a long history of providing highly curated in-person and virtual events designed to deeply engage attendees and amplify the development of professional networks. Throughout the 100-plus year history of the UPCEA annual conference, the organization has provided high-quality content across areas of practice relevant to professional, continuing, and distance education as well as a series of mentorship programs, such as opt-in assignments as conference mentors (or buddies) and a special track for emerging leaders in which midlevel professionals who aspire to more senior roles are provided with opportunities to connect with peers, network with senior professionals, and dive deeply into skill development. UPCEA's annual regional conferences are smaller, more accessible events where new and midlevel members have the opportunity to participate in emerging leader cohorts, small groups of members who, like participants in OLC's Institute for Emerging Leadership in Online Learning, commit to a lengthier engagement to spur their professional development and expand their networks.

UPCEA has invested significantly in a series of resources designed to coalesce attention for and build community around the service of the adult learner, primarily through online and distance education. In 2012, UPCEA leaders began the development of the Center for Online Leadership. Concurrent with those efforts, a group of leaders produced a framework for what makes online initiatives excellent, respected, and essential to their communities (UPCEA, 2017). These hallmarks for online leadership offer a snapshot of what constitutes excellence as well as self-assessments that allow individuals and teams to assess their online unit's activities regarding online teaching and learning in a shared, ongoing pursuit of quality.

In 2017, the Center for Online Leadership was reconceptualized as the NCOE, to reflect a more ecumenical approach to the online community, which is inclusive of other entities that inform a holistic approach to online enterprises. Accordingly, NCOE also promotes community through a host of programs, most notably, the Summit for Online Leadership and Administration + Roundtable (SOLA+R). Now in its fifth year, the SOLA+R event convenes the key leaders directly engaged in the management of online enterprises to define and develop strategies for online learning reflective of institutional priorities and the organization of centralized and decentralized online operations at colleges and universities. Attendees focus on groundbreaking models of successful leadership development, enabling professionals to foster a culture of innovation, creativity, and curiosity throughout their organizations along with policy issues that can have far-reaching impacts on institutions and the online learners they serve.

SOLA+R also features the Online Leadership Roundtable, a body of chief online learning officers and senior leaders responsible for leveraging the strategic potential of online learning, which meets annually in person as a forum to discuss issues related to leadership, strategy, management, and public policy. In 2016, UPCEA launched a special community for higher education instructional design teams (instructional designers, multimedia developers, and team administrators) as a counterpart to the chief online learning officers and in recognition of the essential role they play in online education. Also housed in the NCOE, the e-Design Collaborative provides networking and professional development for the growing community of professionals who are interested in best practices for online teaching and learning and personal development as leaders.

When not attending the national and regional events listed previously, online leaders connect with other UPCEA members through the association's dynamic online collaborative networking platform, which supports vigorous peer-to-peer teaching and learning. This tool supports informal, on-demand learning and dialogue in an open forum accessible to more than 5,000 members involved in professional, continuing, and online education for the purpose of lively, informative, and critical discourse. A unique feature of this forum is the inclusion of corporate members, which provides a camaraderie that makes the staff and faculty of UPCEA member institutions all the richer.

The UPCEA Center for Research and Strategy has delivered actionable market research across the changing higher education landscape and peer consulting for nearly a decade. By regularly involving the membership in benchmarking efforts, the center positions UPCEA members as a community of inquiry through timely data and actionable research, making them indispensable to their campus communities. The center also works in partnership with educational technology companies and marketers to produce research to support the professional development needs of professionals who are eager to interact on emerging practices and new knowledge.

The UPCEA became a founding member of the National Adult Learner Coalition in 2017. It shares this distinction with the Council for Adult and Experiential Learning, the OLC, and the Presidents' Forum. Through a grant from the Lumina Foundation, the National Adult Learner Coalition unites the voices of the leading organizations focused on the adult learner agenda and advocates for the expansion of postsecondary education and credentialing opportunities that will strengthen our communities, regions, and national economy. Many of these opportunities are supported through online learning and address the needs of a growing adult learner audience. The coalition connects the staff and faculty at nearly 1,000 higher education institutions to provide new professional development opportunities focused on innovative directions such as competency-based education, prior learning assessment, and alternative credentialing. This collaboration is further informed by the thoughtful and purpose-driven work supported by the WCET, whose efforts are discussed in the next section.

WCET

WCET has a long and successful history in fostering communities through collaborative projects, information sharing, and networking among some of the country's most established and innovative postsecondary institutions. The cooperative was founded in 1989 by the Western Interstate Commission for Higher Education (WICHE) to meet a growing need to integrate distance learning and educational technology into the academic services of higher education institutions in the western region. From its western roots, the work of WCET has grown to serve members across the United States, Canada, and beyond.

WCET is the leader in the practice, policy, and advocacy of technology-enhanced learning in higher education. WCET is a national, member-driven, nonprofit, which brings together colleges and universities, higher education organizations, and companies to collectively improve the quality and reach of e-learning programs.

WCET is a community in the purest sense of the word: a group of like-minded individuals working toward a common goal. It has been compared to a modern-day barn raising where community members lift up the scaffolding of a building, or an e-learning technology, sharing lessons learned to help smooth the next integration. WCET fosters community through virtual in-person events, special interest groups, demonstration projects, and collaborative projects. WCET members interact through a members-only e-mail list where members can post questions and receive nearly immediate answers from other members who have expertise and experience implementing technology for teaching and learning. Additionally, WCET provides just-in-time learning through its Frontiers blog, research reports, and talking points publications.

Another example of this community is the WCET State Authorization Network, a membership service for those seeking to comply with state authorization regulations related to the provision of online and distance courses and programs. WCET provides training on state regulations, access to experts, and strategies on meeting state requirements and maintains a community of practitioners among participants to share effective practices and latest developments. The network is based on the premise that "expecting each institution to navigate authorization regulations in every state is highly inefficient. Working cooperatively, institutions can share the burden" (WICHE, n.d., para. 3).

In the past, WCET has launched and fostered community by incubating innovative programs such as the International Association for K–12 Online Learning, and the Predictive Analytics Reporting framework, which now offers analytics through the Hobson company platform (par.hobsons.com) as a service to the academic research community, which spotlights research on distance education.

In 2017, WCET joined GlobalMindED to create a digital inclusion award to recognize the significant impact technology can have when engaging first-generation learners with new ideas and perspectives. Also, WCET launched the WCET Z Initiative in 2017, which connects institution-level open educational resource champions, legislators, state systems of higher education, educational technologists, and national open educational resource leaders. The Z Initiative is focused on research, practices, and policies promoting the adoption, implementation, scalability, and sustainability of open educational resources. Students can attend courses and earn degrees that have no-cost textbooks and course materials.

WCET maintains a collegial spirit by embracing its place as a boutique organization focusing on leadership in technology-enhanced higher education. Intentionality in crafting events, virtual and in person, allows members to build lasting relationships with not only the organization but also other higher education leaders. Although small, the community is inclusive of all types of institutions and organizations using technology to improve higher education. Like UPCEA, corporate members have the same weight as institutional members in the WCET community as they all bring value to the conversation with their differences in experiences and voices.

The Landscape of Professional Development

If you look across the organizations discussed in this chapter and compare membership lists, you will see that some institutions belong to all three. We argue that this is not administrative bloat or duplication of services, often derided in higher education, but rather illustrates the unique qualities that each organization brings and the cooperative nature in our work with each other. The three organizations described in this chapter worked on research to identify the modern online learner for the public and for public policy makers. Collaboration makes all three organizations stronger and demonstrates the strength of the greater online and technology-enhanced learning communities.

Informal Digital Learning Communities

Although the three organizations discussed in this chapter provide a robust and comprehensive framework, this discussion would be incomplete without mentioning the informal opportunities that support learning and innovative practices of online professionals. There is a vast array of opportunities to engage in informal digital learning communities such as formal conference gatherings where informal communities meet and continue their gatherings and discussions through social media. Other opportunities are available on social media and are open to all. A few notable sources include Virtually Connecting (virtuallyconnecting.org), podcasts, and social media communities.

Virtually Connecting

The volunteer founders of Virtually Connecting created this informal community to enliven virtual attendance at academic conferences. The community uses emerging technologies to connect onsite conference attendees and presenters with virtual attendees in small groups, while often simultaneously broadcasting the experience live to anyone who would like to watch. For virtual attendees, the feeling of being in the know through hallway conversations or coffee breaks can be lost. Virtually Connecting aims to break down that barrier between those who are attending remotely and those on site, no matter where in the world the conference is held. Virtually Connecting also maintains a strong Twitter back channel, holding relevant conversations using the hashtag #vconnecting.

Podcasts

There are multiple podcasts on a variety of topics pertinent to the digital learning field. A few worth mentioning for their relevance to online learning are #3wedu, Research in Action, To a Degree: A Higher Ed Podcast, and TOPcast.

The podcast and online community #3wedu (3wedu.wordpress.com) features notable leaders in online learning. The monthly live video podcast is supported by a Twitter back channel and a community Google Doc.

Participants in #3wedu examine topics relevant to women in higher education, with a special focus on those working in innovation and research. The podcast has broached such issues as gender equality in pay, dress, and access to resources for conducting research and implementing innovation. Additionally, #3wedu leaders introduced topics of discussion surrounding self-care, self-promotion, and mentoring. These topics are important to all women in higher education, however, in innovative higher education, where we bridge the relationship of technology and education, gender inequity can be even more pronounced. Understanding the implications of the gendered nature of technology is important for those innovating in higher education. All these conversations happen over a glass of wine, hence the full name of the podcast, Women Who Wine in Education, or #3wedu as it is listed in various podcasting directories. At conferences, the #3wedu community gathers to introduce the group to newcomers and continue community-building efforts for those more familiar with the podcast.

The Research in Action (ecampus.oregonstate.edu/research/podcast) podcast is hosted by Kathryn E. Linder, research director for Ecampus at Oregon State University, and features researchers from across the country who discuss different facets of innovative research, including research design and methodology. The podcast is funded by the Oregon State University Ecampus with a goal of building community among higher education researchers.

To a Degree (postsecondary.gatesfoundation.org/podcasts), moderated by Casey Green, founding director of the Campus Computing Project, is the Bill and Melinda Gates Foundation Postsecondary Success unit's monthly podcast that "highlights the people, institutions, and organizations that are working to provide all students with a high-quality and affordable postsecondary experience, especially those at the greatest risk of being left out" (Bill and Melinda Gates Foundation, 2017, para. 1).

The University of Central Florida's Teaching Online Podcast (cdl.ucf .edu/teach/resources/topcast), or TOPcast as it is listed in podcast directories, is another monthly offering featuring professionals in the digital learning field. With hosts Tom Cavanaugh and Kelvin Thompson, guests discuss a variety of topics relevant to online learning. Podcasts such as these offer the opportunity to learn from others in an informal setting.

Social Media Communities

Informal conversations can be a great way to build community online. In the academic community, one popular way to do this is through threaded Twitter chats, using a hashtag *#protocol*. Although some hashtags remain the same across time (e.g., #3wedu) others pop up to discuss campus events or promote community gatherings. The best way to find the Twitter chats relevant to your innovative practice are to simply search Twitter for key words such as #highered or #edtech. Another great way to locate and join Twitter chats is to check the event feeds for the formal and informal organizations mentioned in this chapter; they all have robust Twitter accounts and may be a good place to begin your search for a Twitter community (@OLCToday, @UPCEA, @wcet_info, @3wedu, @vconnecting, @topcastnow, @RIA_podcast).

Making the Most of Your Professional Development Community

To make the most of your professional community, you must engage. Find your tribe and seek people who are studying, trying, learning, and doing things you are doing or you want to be involved in. To do this most effectively, take time to reflect on your comfort level with participating in a community, your ability to balance your commitment to your community with your work and life commitments, and what your goals are in finding a community. As you're exploring different communities, formal and informal, take time to make personal connections. Stretch your networking muscle and make personal connections with others at virtual and physical events. Do not be afraid to insert yourself into an ongoing conversation, whether through a Twitter back channel or walking up to a table full of new faces. Once you have found your community, get involved. Volunteer for committees, work on special projects, or lead an informal, no-host dinner group at an on-site meeting.

Also remember when joining a community, it is important to think about what you can contribute to the community as well as what you can gain from participating in the community. Finding the right community or communities as you traverse your career is also valuable to consider. Changing positions or simply changing the focus of your current position may prompt you to consider changing your engagement in a community or even adding a new community to your focus. Remaining agile concerning your professional development trajectory will allow you to participate in ways that make a difference personally and professionally.

Whether formal or informal, communities are dynamic and reliant on you and others to expand them, shape them, and drive them. As an homage to an innovator in American history, apply President John F. Kennedy's words to your community: "Ask not what your country can do for you—ask what you can do for your country" (Kennedy, 1961).

References

Bill and Melinda Gates Foundation. (2017). *To a Degree: A highered podcast.* Retrieved from https://postsecondary.gatesfoundation.org/podcasts/

Kennedy, J. F. (1961). *Ask not what your country can do for you . . .* Retrieved from https://www.jfklibrary.org/Education/Teachers/Curricular-Resources/Elementary-School-Curricular-Materials/Ask-Not.aspx

Kentor, H. (2015). Distance education and the evolution of online learning in the United States. *Curriculum and Teaching Dialogue, 17*(1/2), pp. 21–34.

Online Learning Consortium. (2017). *Our quality framework.* Retrieved from https://onlinelearningconsortium.org/about/quality-framework-five-pillars/

Picciano, A. G. (2013). *Pioneering higher education's digital future: An evaluation of the Alfred P. Sloan Foundation's Anytime, Anyplace Learning program* (1992–2012). New York, NY: City University of New York. Retrieved from https://aalp-sloan-report.gc.cuny.edu/timeline/

University Professional Continuing Education Association. (2017). *Hallmarks of excellence in online leadership.* Retrieved from http://upcea.edu/resources/hallmarks-online/

Western Interstate Commission for Higher Education Cooperative for Educational Technologies. (n.d.). *State authorization network.* Retrieved from http://wcet.wiche.edu/initiatives/state-authorization-network

Creating Your Innovation Action Plan

Kathryn E. Linder and Rolin Moe

I t can be challenging to identify the concrete steps needed to innovate individually or in one's unit or larger organization. In this conclusion, we offer a series of guiding questions to help you apply the information from this book to actionable steps you can immediately begin to implement. These questions will also assist you in synthesizing the information from the previous chapters so it can be applied to your unique context.

Guiding Questions

The questions provided here can be referred to as many times as needed as you grow and develop as an innovator. We also know that successful innovation at the institutional level frequently happens through the work of individuals collaborating together on a larger vision. Thus, throughout this conclusion, we invite you to look at your next steps for innovation from the individual and organizational levels.

Defining Innovation

The complexity of innovation becomes evident when we think about the concept's history as well as its modern usage. When the word is used as an abstract concept, it lacks conceptual understanding and becomes a transmitter for hope in lieu of an agent for practical change. Being innovative and promoting innovation in education requires understanding the multiple contexts in which we innovate and discuss innovation on an individual as well as a societal level. Use the following questions to develop a concrete definition for how you think of innovation in your context.

- Question: Using the chapters of this book as a resource, what are the most important components making up innovation in education? What do you see as integral to the concept of *innovation*? Identify any historical uses of the term or literary references that help shape this understanding.
  - Next steps or action items: What actions would help you move forward with this?
  - Sample action: Write a personal definition of *innovation*. This definition might describe the meaning of the word as you use it, either in general or specific to your personal work.
- Question: How does your organization or institution view innovation? If a statement exists, analyze it: What aspects of innovation mentioned in this book drive your statement, and what is left out? If there is no statement regarding innovation, analyze existing documentation on the topic, searching for the same drivers and omissions. What key findings do you think determine how your organization sees innovation?
  - Next steps or action items: What actions would help you move forward with this?
  - Sample action: If there is no existing mission statement on innovation at your institution, draft a brief paragraph outlining the relationship of the institution's strategic vision and how innovation supports those objectives. If there is an existing mission statement, is the statement indicative of existing practice? If not, how would you merge the existing practices of the institution with the stated vision to best support innovation?

Stumbling Blocks

In the first stage of development, it is important to identify any potential stumbling blocks that might hinder the creation and implementation of innovation projects. Reviewing the chapters throughout this book, identify some of the challenges and stumbling blocks the contributors discussed and their solutions. Then use the following questions to think about potential obstacles to innovation at the individual and organizational levels at your institution.

- Question: Based on what you have read in this book, can you identify any stumbling blocks with innovation for you as an individual?
  - Next steps or action items: What actions would help you move forward with this?

○ Sample action: Identify an individual who has overcome this stumbling block and schedule an informational phone call to learn more about the situation.

- Question: Based on what you have read in this book, can you identify any stumbling blocks for innovation in your unit or larger organization?
  ○ Next steps or action items: What actions would help you move forward with this?
  ○ Sample action: Identify an organization that has overcome this stumbling block and schedule an informational phone call with a leader there to learn more about the situation.

Areas for Professional Development

If you are reading this book, it is possible that you are already engaging in innovative endeavors at your institution and perhaps even leading those projects. It is also possible that you are just getting started with thinking about your role in the innovative vision of your unit or organization. Use the questions in this section to think about one or two areas where you think you would benefit from additional training, information, or guidance. You will also want to identify the one or two areas of expertise that would most benefit your organization.

- Question: Based on what you have read in this book, can you identify the most important areas of professional development for you as an individual?
  ○ Next steps or action items: What actions would help you move forward with this?
  ○ Sample action: Research the books, webinars, conferences, training, consultants, or other resources that would help you learn more about this particular topic or issue. (The resources in chapter 8 on professional development are an excellent starting point.)
- Question: Based on what you have read in this book, can you identify the most important areas of professional development for your unit or larger organization?
  ○ Next steps or action items: What actions would help you move forward with this?
  ○ Sample action: Research the group training, conferences, or consultants that would allow you and others in your organization to learn about this topic or issue together.

Areas of Innovative Strength

As useful as it is to identify gaps or areas of further development on the creation and implementation of innovation for you and your institution, it is equally important to identify the strengths that can be applied toward an innovative vision. Use the questions in this section to determine your pockets of strength, including certain institutional stakeholders' supporting the idea, potential funding opportunities, or individual traits such as brainstorming that will lend themselves well to innovation efforts.

- Question: What areas of innovative strength can you identify for you as an individual? Consider the different areas of strength you can offer personally and professionally.
  - Next steps or action items: What actions would help you move forward with this?
  - Sample action: Reflect on how the areas of innovative strength you have identified have served you in the past. What have these strengths allowed you to accomplish? What examples can you provide of positive results from using these strengths?
- Question: What areas of innovative strength can you identify in your unit or larger organization? In other words, what will help your organization engage in more innovation or implement innovations more successfully?
  - Next steps or action items: What actions would help you move forward with this?
  - Sample action: Reflect on how the areas of innovative strength you have identified have served your institution in the past. What have these strengths allowed your institution to accomplish? What examples can you provide of positive results for your institution from using these strengths?

Innovation Collaborators

One of the key takeaways from the book is the importance of purposeful approaches to projects, processes, and procedures. Innovation requires a culture of support that provides the opportunity to work alongside people with a myriad of expertise. Use the questions from this section to identify the people, departments, and organizations (inside and outside the institution) that will be necessary to support and sustain innovation. Also consider the potential obstacles in working with different people, departments, and organizations and how to proactively support collaboration.

- Question: Identify a specific innovation project or process you plan to work on. Where are opportunities for collaboration? Be as specific as possible: people, departments, outside agencies, and so on.
  - Next steps or action items: What actions would help you move forward with this?
  - Sample action: Thinking about an innovation you wish to pursue, identify what would ensure its success. From there, make a list of potential partners for the project or process.
- Question: Are there people, departments, or outside organizations you should work with to be successful in your innovation but have presented challenges to innovation in the past? Identify any common struggles or obstacles you would have with these potential partners.
  - Next steps or action items: What actions would help you move forward with this?
  - Sample action: Think specifically about a potential partner you struggle to work with. Consider the innovation from your partner's perspective, their existing staffing, and workflow. What differences do you see from your initial struggles and the project from this partner's vision? How could you work to address the situation and strengthen the working relationship?

Next Steps and Action Items

Based on your responses to the previous questions, you may already have the beginning of a list of potential next steps or action items to continue your growth and development with innovating online. Draft a list of your next steps and action items here.

- Question: Of the next steps and action items you have identified, which should be completed first?
  - Sample action: Schedule in your priority actions into your calendar for the next week or month.
- Question: Of the next steps and action items you have identified, which involve other people? Can you identify the other people involved?
  - Sample action: Contact the people on your next steps and action items list to schedule a strategy session.

Recognizing that each institutional and individual context is different, this scaffolding does not provide a formula or set of steps to achieve innovation. Rather, it provides a foundation for the ongoing exploration and understanding of the elements of personal and organizational innovation. Starting with a contextualization of the innovation concept, this set of guiding questions and the preceding chapters seek to encourage reflection and action on current and emergent practices in online education. It is up to the faculty, staff, librarians, administrators, instructional designers, and all other members of your educational community to determine what is most appropriate for the innovative projects and products at your institution. We look forward to seeing increased engagement in the potential of online innovations to create unique and sustainable practices for the future of education.

EDITOR AND CONTRIBUTORS

Editor

Kathryn E. Linder is the research director for Ecampus at Oregon State University. She earned her BA in English literature and creative writing from Whitworth University and her MA and PhD in women's studies from the Ohio State University. Linder is the author of *Rampage Violence Narratives* (Lexington Books, 2014), *The Blended Course Design Workbook* (Stylus Publishing, 2016), and *Managing Your Professional Identity Online* (Stylus Publishing, 2018). She is also the editor of the *New Directions for Teaching and Learning: Hybrid Teaching and Learning* and the series editor for Thrive Online published by Stylus Publishing. As part of her work at Ecampus, Linder also hosts the weekly Research in Action podcast on topics and issues related to research in higher education.

Contributors

Deborah Adair, PhD, is the executive director and chief operating officer of Quality Matters (QM), an international nonprofit organization providing a scalable quality assurance system for online and blended learning within and across organizations. Used by more than 1,100 institutions spanning K–12, higher education, and professional and corporate training, QM's tools and processes allow administrators, educators and education professionals to share resources and knowledge as they work to improve technology-enhanced education and meet QM's nationally recognized standards. Adair has more than 30 years' experience in higher education, teaching and administration, and nonprofit leadership and management consulting. She has been in a leadership role at QM since 2007 and has served on advisory bodies for the Western Interstate Commission for Higher Education Cooperative for Educational Technologies, the National University Technology Network, the Presidents' Forum, and Credential Engine. As an expert in quality assurance for online education, Adair is a frequent keynote speaker, presenter, and author.

Nelson C. Baker, PhD, is the dean of professional education at the Georgia Institute of Technology and associate professor in the university's School of Civil and Environmental Engineering. As dean, Baker leads a multifaceted operation including the Global Learning Center, Georgia Tech–Savannah, the Language Institute, and Georgia Tech's extensive professional education programs in subjects related to science, technology, engineering, and mathematics and business. Baker also oversees educational outreach programs and serves as the interface between Georgia Tech's professional education activities and the industries, corporations, government agencies, and professional societies that benefit from them. Under Baker's leadership, Georgia Tech professional education has steadily expanded, now reaching more than 33,000 learners and 2,800 organizations each year from more than half the world's countries. Baker's work on the impact of technology on students' learning has generated recognition such as the W. M. Keck Foundation Award for Engineering Teaching Excellence, a National Science Foundation National Young Investigator Award, the Best Paper Award from the American Society of Civil Engineers' *Journal of Computing in Civil Engineering*, the Georgia Tech Outstanding Innovative Use of Education Technology Award, and the Georgia Tech W. Roane Beard Outstanding Teacher Award. Currently Baker serves as the secretary general of the International Association of Continuing Engineering Education and also serves as the president-elect for the University Professional Continuing Education Association.

Alfonso Bradoch is the director of the Academic Programs Management and Data Analytics unit for Oregon State University's Ecampus, with more than 6,000 students, 32 degree programs, and more than 700 online courses. With Ecampus since 2005, he is responsible for services to enhance the effectiveness and efficiency of Ecampus and its academic partner units, ensuring that policies and processes are in alignment and supportive of the distant education mission of the institution. Bradoch completed his formal education earning his bachelor's degree in philosophy (epistemology, Loyola-Marymount University) and master's degree in psychology (experimental and social, California State University, Los Angeles). Over a nearly 30-year career in higher education, he has served in leadership positions at institutions of differing sizes and educational scope in Washington and Oregon. His professional experience in higher education administration is in financial aid, admissions (domestic and international), and units focusing on student success initiatives.

Rovy Branon is vice provost for Continuum College at the University of Washington. In his role, he oversees more than 200 staff serving 55,000 learners each year through professional and continuing education, international English language programs, summer quarter, Osher Lifelong Learning Institute, and online programs. Branon has more than 25 years of experience in educational media, online technology, and distance education. Prior to his role at the University of Washington, Branon was associate dean for online learning at the University of Wisconsin Extension. He built his first online class in 1995 and was codeveloper on a patented electronic textbook delivery technology in 2012. Branon has spoken at more than 100 national and international events and has published more than 30 papers, book chapters, and reports. Branon maintains an active social media presence with his educationally focused Twitter feed, which has more than 20,000 followers. His advocacy for increasing access to higher education and workforce development has also been featured in traditional media, including CBS TechRepublic, Fox Business, GeekWire, Portland NBC affiliate KGW, *Seattle Times*, *USA Today*, and numerous regional publications. He holds a doctorate from Indiana University in instructional systems technology, where he also taught online graduate courses for more than 15 years.

Lois Brooks serves as vice provost for information and technology and chief information officer at the University of Wisconsin–Madison, where she provides vision, leadership, and advocacy for the effective application of information technologies to the instructional, research, and service missions of the university. Brooks has more than 30 years of experience in higher education, previously serving as vice provost for information and technology and chief information officer at Oregon State University and director of academic technology at Stanford University. She is active nationally in the higher education community and has served in governance roles with the Northwest Academic Computing Consortium, Unizin, EDUCAUSE Learning Initiative, IMS Global, and Internet2. During her tenure at Stanford she cofounded the Sakai Foundation, serving on the board of directors and later as executive director. Brooks holds an MBA from Columbia University; an MBA from the University of California, Berkeley; and a BS from the University of San Francisco.

Jill Buban is the chief academic officer at Unizin. Buban oversees research efforts that use the Unizin Data Platform, member engagement, and marketing and communications. Prior to this position, Buban was the senior director of research and innovation at the Online Learning Consortium where she oversaw the Research Center for Digital Learning and Leadership and the organization's peer-reviewed journal, *Online Learning*, for which she also served as a special issue editor. Buban has provided multiple keynotes and presentations nationally and internationally. Before stepping into this role, Buban was the assistant provost for research and innovation at Post

University, where she oversaw all aspects of digital learning initiatives. While at Post, Buban served as the dean of the School of Education and was academic program manager for the master of education. This followed a position in academic affairs at State University of New York Empire State College. Buban is a member of the Senior Leadership Group for the Association of Chief Academic Officers Digital Fellows and the Board of Directors at the National University Technology Networks and volunteers with several local organizations in her community. Buban earned her PhD in educational studies with a specialization in adult learning from Lesley University. She holds an MS in curriculum and instruction from State University of New York College at Plattsburgh, and a BA in history from the University of New Hampshire. Buban has received several awards for her accomplishments, including being named to the 2017 class of Online Learning Consortium Fellows, Best in Track Award from the Sloan-C International Conference on Online Learning in 2011, Emerging Scholar for the Society for the Study of Emerging Adulthood in 2012, and the *Hartford Business Journal*'s 40 under 40 achievement in 2014.

Thomas Cavanagh, PhD, is vice provost for digital learning at the University of Central Florida. In this role he oversees all classroom technology and the distance learning strategy, policies, and practices of one of the nation's largest universities, where online learning is a key element for fulfilling the institutional mission. In his career, Cavanagh has administered e-learning development for academic (public and private) and industrial (Fortune 500, government, and military) audiences. He has been recognized with a number of awards including the U.S. States Distance Learning Administration's Outstanding Leadership Award and was named an Online Learning Consortium Fellow. He is a frequent speaker at industry conferences and often consults with other institutions regarding their online learning strategies. He is active in the higher education community and serves on a number of national advisory boards. He is also an award-winning author of several mystery novels.

Luke Dowden is the chief online learning officer and associate vice chancellor of academic success at the Alamo Colleges District. Through Alamo Colleges Online, he leads and supports capacity-building initiatives at all five colleges so each may gain a greater market share of online learners in their service areas. Prior to joining Alamo Colleges Online, Dowden founded the Office of Distance Learning at the University of Louisiana at Lafayette in 2010 and served as its director for eight years. Under Dowden's leadership, the Office of Distance Learning earned the 2013 Online Learning

Consortium's Award for Excellence in Faculty Development for Online Teaching. Dowden was honored in 2014 as the inaugural recipient of the Online Learning Consortium Bruce N. Chaloux Award for Early Career Excellence in Online Education. Prior to joining the University of Louisiana at Lafayette, Dowden founded the Division of Accelerated Learning at Bossier Parish Community College. During this time, the Louisiana Board of Regents tapped him to found and lead the Center for Adult Learning in Louisiana. As the center's executive director of CALL from 2008 to 2013, he worked primarily with 6 community colleges and regional universities to create and launch more than 18 accelerated online degree programs, introduce prior learning assessment policies and strategies, and coordinate marketing the programs statewide to more than 500,000 adults with some college and no degree. Dowden earned a bachelor's degree in history and a master's degree in adult education from Northwestern State University before earning his doctorate of education in higher education administration in 2009 from Nova Southeastern University. He is a 2010 graduate of the Penn State and Online Learning Consortium Institute for Emerging Leadership in Online Learning.

Jessica DuPont is the executive director of market development and the student experience in the division of Ecampus at Oregon State University. With 20 years of experience in higher education marketing and leadership, DuPont has extensive experience in market research and strategic marketing planning to help ensure that programs developed meet consumer and industry demand. She has led teams to win numerous marketing awards from the University Professional and Continuing Education Association and the American Marketing Association. DuPont has presented at numerous national conferences and has also served as the vice chair for research and emerging trends for the University Professional and Continuing Education Association's marketing network and on its board for Region West. She earned her BA in English and French from the University of Wisconsin and an MBA from Oregon State University. Her favorite early career experience was teaching English in the Peace Corps in Romania.

Dianna Fisher retired from Oregon State University after working there for 17 years, most recently as the director of Open Oregon State. Previously she directed the course development unit of Ecampus, a group of award-winning multimedia programmers and course designers. Fisher is passionate about lowering costs for students, especially in the area of open textbooks and other no-cost course materials, and served on several advisory boards outside the university, working with tribal governments and statewide open education advocates. Fisher holds a BA in history, an MA in anthropology and women's studies, and a PhD from the College of Forestry at Oregon State University.

Amy Claire Heitzman is the deputy chief executive officer and chief learning officer for the University Professional and Continuing Education Association. With degrees in art history from the University of Michigan and the University of Chicago, Heitzman began her career in museum education, developing programs and training museum educators at various university art museums, including the Art Institute of Chicago and the Dallas Museum of Art. After having served as education director for the Meadows Museum on the campus of Southern Methodist University (SMU), her interest in adult learners led her to the directorship in 2002 of SMU's continuing education unit. As executive director of continuing and professional education, Heitzman directed a new strategic vision for the unit, effectively doubling the number of programs offered and students served, increasing the university's capacity to more deeply engage with its community. While at SMU, Heitzman served in various leadership roles including board membership in the SMU Staff Association and the Hegi Family Career Center and as an appointed member of the Presidential Council for Community Engagement and the Faculty and Staff Committee of the Second Century Capital Campaign. During her time at SMU she earned graduate certificates in marketing and nonprofit leadership, as well as an MEd. Heitzman earned her doctorate in higher education administration at the University of Texas at Austin in 2014. Her dissertation focused on female student veterans in higher education. Heitzman writes and presents on examinations of nontraditional learners; the experiences of student veterans, particularly female student veterans; and comparative studies of international higher education systems. Heitzman has been active in various professional organizations throughout her career, including serving on the Executive Committee of the University Professional and Continuing Education Association Board of Directors, the InsideTrack National Advisory Board, the George W. Bush Institute's Military Service Institute Education and Training Task Force, and the Higher Education Advisory Group of the Credential Engine. She also served as a reviewer for the Chief Learning Officer LearningElite program, the Student Veterans of America National Conference, and the Association for the Study of Higher Education Annual Conference.

James Hilton is vice provost for academic innovation and university librarian and dean of libraries at the University of Michigan, where he leads one of the world's largest and most innovative library systems and spearheads the development of campuswide strategies, policies, and programs on educational technology. A national leader in technology issues on higher education, he has led, championed, and fostered technology initiatives that cross boundaries among institutions and among academic and information technology units. He was an early supporter of the Sakai Project, a collaborative effort to create open software that advances teaching, learning, and research; provided crucial early support to multi-institutional efforts to deploy technology to further education, research, and preservation, including Internet2 NET+ and DuraSpace; and led the creation of the Digital Preservation Network to develop a collective ecosystem to protect the scholarly record, including the growing amount of born-digital scholarship, for future generations. Recently Hilton helped spearhead the development and launch of the Unizin Consortium, a partnership of universities that is empowering participating institutions to exert greater control over the infrastructure, content, and data that drive and emerge from the expanding digital learning landscape. He has served on many boards, including Internet2, DuraSpace, Digital Preservation Network, and the HathiTrust Board of Governors. Hilton received a BA in psychology from the University of Texas at Austin in 1981 and a PhD in social psychology from Princeton University in 1985.

Nina B. Huntemann is the senior director of academics and research at edX. Prior to joining edX, Huntemann spent 15 years in the university classroom—on campus and online—teaching graduate and undergraduate courses in communication and media studies. She received her doctoral degree in communications from the University of Massachusetts Amherst.

Dave King is professor emeritus at Oregon State University. King served as special assistant for innovation in the provost's office from 2016 to 2017. Prior to that he was associate provost for outreach and engagement at Oregon State University and professor in the College of Agricultural Sciences. His responsibilities in the provost's office included Ecampus, Open Oregon State, Summer Session, Professional and Continuing Education, and Extension and Experiment Station Communications. King was a member of the Unizin consortium's board of directors from its inception in 2014 until 2017. In addition, King served on the senior executive team for the Division of Outreach and Engagement at Oregon State. From 1998 to 2006 King was executive director of the Indiana Higher Education Telecommunication System, a consortium of 40 Indiana colleges and universities, and chief executive officer of the Indiana College Network. King also served as the acting director of communications (1991 to 1993) for the Cooperative State

Research Service of the U.S. Department of Agriculture in Washington DC. King has a track record of international communications and distance education program development in Mexico, Honduras, Nicaragua, Costa Rica, Kenya, and China. King has an MA from the University of Oregon in journalism (1983) and a BA from California State University, Chico in mass communication (1972).

Rolin Moe is an assistant professor and the director of academic innovation at Seattle Pacific University. He earned his BA in English literature from Centenary College; his MA in radio, TV, and film from the University of Texas; and his EdD in learning technologies from Pepperdine University. At Seattle Pacific University, Rolin works alongside faculty, staff, and administration to contextualize academic innovations, provide research and development for initiatives, and incorporate successful projects into processes and operations. Rolin practices innovation in his practitioner work, most notably through a three-year partnership with the Online Learning Consortium by hosting an Innovation Installation at its annual Innovate Conference, a critical conversation where the space is scaffolded as an innovation artifact to best support the emergent conversations. Rolin's publications cross academic and mainstream presses: his work has been included in *Learning, Media & Technology*; *Current Issues in Emerging eLearning*; *Emergence & Innovation in Digital Learning* (Athabasca University Press, 2016); EDUCAUSE; and the NPR blog *MindShift*.

Cali M.K. Morrison is associate dean of alternative learning at American Public University System. Previously Morrison was the assistant director of communications and analysis and project director of Transparency by Design at the Western Interstate Commission for Higher Education's Cooperative for Educational Technologies, where she became interested in studying adult learners and accountability. Current research interests include competency-based education, microcredentials, and the future of learning and work. Morrison holds a BA in public relations from Western Kentucky University, an MEd in adult and higher education from Montana State University, an online graduate certificate in women's studies from Western Kentucky University, and an EdD in higher education administration from Montana State University. Prior to joining the Cooperative for Educational Technologies, Morrison worked at Montana State University for more than 7 years in various positions including managing 13 federal grants for the Extension Service Housing and Environmental Health unit, administering a $1.6 million Howard Hughes Medical Institute grant to improve undergraduate biomedical education and access to research opportunities, advising students, and serving as the adviser for Greek organizations, among other appointments. Morrison lives near Bozeman, Montana, with her husband, two daughters, and dogs. She is active in the community, especially with the Child Advancement Project mentoring and Girls For A Change programs.

Karen L. Pedersen currently serves as the dean for global campus at Kansas State University. Previously, Pedersen served as the chief knowledge officer for the Online Learning Consortium, where she led thought leader initiatives related to learning innovation, quality enhancement, community engagement and leadership development, institutional transformation, and policy advocacy. Throughout her career she has led award-winning off-campus and online learning units focusing on engaging cross-institutional academic operations while pursuing enrollment growth and learner success outcomes. Other professional experiences include launching more than 25 innovative online degree programs and numerous certificate programs, serving on the launch team for a competency-based education initiative, leading a systemwide enrollment management transformation, and expanding academic partnerships with each of the military branches, small businesses, and corporations, community colleges, and internationally in Brazil, Hong Kong, Indonesia, Malaysia, and Singapore. Prior to starting her administrative career, Pedersen served as a full-time faculty member and currently serves as a faculty member for the Online Learning Consortium Institute for Emerging Leadership in Online Learning. She holds a BS and an MS from the University of Nebraska–Lincoln and a PhD from Oklahoma State University.

Phil Regier is university dean for educational initiatives and chief executive officer of EdPlus at Arizona State University. Regier is responsible for expanding the university's digital immersion program and advancing the university's leadership role in education innovation. During his tenure as dean, the fully online student population has grown from 400 to 38,000, and the number of online degree programs has grown from 6 to 180. Today, the university's online programs use more than 200 technologies, and the university is a coconvener of the ASU + GSV (Arizona State University and Global Silicon Valley) Education Innovation Summit, the largest and most recognized assembly of education technology entrepreneurs, investors, and users in the world. A philosophy major and math minor, Regier earned his BA from St. John's College in Santa Fe, New Mexico. He also holds a PhD in accountancy from the University of Illinois at Urbana–Champaign.

Shannon Riggs serves as executive director for Oregon State University's Ecampus, in charge of course development and learning innovation. She holds a master's degree in professional writing and began her career in higher education teaching writing in face-to-face, hybrid, and online modalities. A passion for online education and course design led to opportunities in faculty development and support, then to instructional design and later to leadership roles in online education. Riggs and her team are the recipients of two awards from the Online Learning Consortium, an Award for Excellence in Faculty Development for Online Teaching, an Effective Practice Award, an Eduventures Innovation Award, and a Western Interstate Commission for Higher Education Cooperative for Educational Technologies WOW Award. Riggs is the professional development lead for the Quality Matters Instructional Design Association and is a member of the Cooperative for Educational Technologies steering committee. Riggs is the author of *Thrive Online: A New Approach for College Educators* (Stylus Publishing, in press).

Kathryn Scheckel has led a variety of strategic initiatives at Arizona State University (ASU), including a transdisciplinary partnership between ASU and Starbucks. At ASU she held a variety of roles from 2012 to 2018, including director of strategic projects in the Office of the President. She also served as special adviser to the chief executive officer of ASU's education technology unit EdPlus. Scheckel has published articles in a variety of peer-reviewed journals including *Neuron* and *The Journal of Law, Medicine and Ethics*. Scheckel holds a BS in molecular biosciences and biotechnology, a BA in piano, and an MA in public policy from ASU, where she was also a Flinn Scholar. She also holds a professional certificate in management from Stanford's Graduate School of Business. She currently works as a consultant at McKinsey & Company.

Kay Shattuck has been actively involved in adult education practice for more than 35 years, initially with adults in transition and since 1999, distance education. In 2002 Shattuck was part of a group of Maryland distance educators awarded a Fund for the Improvement of Secondary Education Grant from the U.S. Department of Education. The resulting program—Quality Matters—is now an international program to improve online education. She continues a leadership position with Quality Matters as the director of research. Shattuck's academic affiliation is with Pennsylvania State University's College of Education, Education and Learning Performance Systems, where she began teaching online with the

World Campus in 2000. She is the editor of *Assuring Quality in Online Education: Practices and Processes at Teaching, Resource, and Program Levels* (Stylus Publishing, 2014) and an associate editor for the *American Journal of Distance Education*.

Lisa L. Templeton serves as associate provost for Oregon State University Ecampus. She provides leadership for units whose collective mission is to provide learners in Oregon and around the world with access to a high-quality education. The division of Ecampus also houses an active Ecampus Research Unit and Open Educational Resources unit. Under her leadership, Ecampus has built a reputation as one of the nation's best providers of online education, delivering more than 1,200 courses and more than 50 degree programs to distance learners in all 50 states and more than 50 countries. Templeton has been with Ecampus since 2000. She is active nationally in the field of online and continuing education and has served on the board of directors for the University Professional and Continuing Education Association. She earned her BS from the Ohio State University, her EdM in Adult Education from Oregon State University, and a certificate from the Institute for Emerging Leadership in Online Education from the Online Learning Consortium and Pennsylvania State University.

Julie Uranis serves as the vice president for Online and Strategic Initiatives at the University Professional Continuing Education Association (UPCEA). In this capacity she is the managing director of the National Council for Online Education. Prior to joining UPCEA, she led the Distance Learning and Continuing and Professional Development units at Western Kentucky University as the director. During her time at Western Kentucky, the university was recognized for distance learning accessibility operations with the 2016 UPCEA Strategic Innovation in Online Education Award and earned consecutive top-five rankings in the *US News and World Report's* list of Best Online Bachelor's Programs. Uranis began her career at Eastern Michigan University, where she held teaching and administrative positions. She continues to serve the university as a part-time instructor in the Leadership and Counseling Department. Uranis earned her BA in history from the University of Michigan–Dearborn and her MS in technology studies, graduate certificate in community college leadership, and PhD in educational leadership, all from Eastern Michigan University. Uranis writes and presents on online administration, professional and continuing education, working with adult learners, bachelor's completion programs for career technical students, and new and emerging technologies. She has been active with various organizations throughout her professional career including the UPCEA Executive Committee and Board of Directors and other volunteer leadership roles, the Association of Continuing Higher Education editorial board of the *Journal of Continuing Higher Education*, the Online Learning Consortium as a reviewer for *Online Learning Journal*, the Kentucky Distance Learning Steering Committee meeting convener and cochair of the 2015 and 2016 Kentucky Convergence Conference, leader of the Competency-Based Education Network's 2015–2016 business and financial model work team, Instructional Management System (IMS) Global, the Blackboard Executive Competency-Based Education Advisory Council, and other regional community groups and higher education associations.

Craig D. Weidemann, vice president for outreach and vice provost for online education emeritus, retired from Pennsylvania State University in 2018 after serving as special assistant to the provost for innovation and education technology initiatives since 2016. After 12 years, he stepped down in January 2016 from his position as vice president for outreach and vice provost for online education, where he led the university's outreach initiatives and the Penn State Online World Campus. He is currently on the Online Learning Consortium board and has served as a board member of the Association of Public and Land-grant Universities, Advisory Council for the University Professional Continuing Education Association Center for Online Leadership and Strategy, the Engagement Scholarship Consortium, the American Distance Education Consortium, and the University Professional Continuing Education Association. Prior to his tenure at Penn State, Weidemann held administrative positions at Johns Hopkins University, the University of Illinois at Urbana–Champaign, and the University of Maryland, Baltimore County. He received his PhD in educational psychology in 1982.

Brad Wheeler is Indiana University's vice president for information technology and chief information officer. He leads university-wide information technology services for eight campuses. He has cofounded and led open source software and service collaborations such as the Sakai Project, Kuali, and the HathiTrust. He also developed the university's eTexts initiative and implemented a cutting-edge delivery model to tackle the high costs of textbooks for students. He cofounded Unizin, a consortium of universities seeking to exert greater control and influence over the digital learning landscape. He is the James H. Rudy Professor of Information Systems in the university's Kelley School of Business.